# THE POKER PLAYER'S GUIDE TO PARENTING

LEAHA HAMMER

Library Tales Publishing

www.LibraryTalesPublishing.com

www.Facebook.com/LibraryTalesPublishing

Copyright © 2025 by Leaha Marie Hammer

All Rights Reserved

Published in New York, New York.

No part of this publication may be reproduced, stored in a retrieval system, or transmitted in any form or by any means, electronic, mechanical, photocopying, recording, scanning, or otherwise, except as permitted under Sections 107 or 108 of the 1976 United States Copyright Act, without the prior written permission of the Publisher. Requests to the Publisher for permission should be addressed to the Legal Department: Legal@LibraryTales.com

**Trademarks:** Library Tales Publishing, Library Tales, the Library Tales Publishing logo, and related trade dress are trademarks or registered trademarks of Library Tales Publishing and/or its affiliates in the United States and other countries, and may not be used without written permission. All other trademarks are the property of their respective owners.

For general information on our other products and services, please contact our Customer Care Department at 1-800-754-5016, or fax 917-463-0892. For technical support, please visit www.LibraryTalesPublishing.com

Library Tales Publishing also publishes its books in a variety of electronic formats. Every content that appears in print is available in electronic books.

9798894410197

Printed in the United States of America

*"Parenting is like a game of poker: you start with high hopes and a solid strategy, but by the end of the day, you're just bluffing your way through bedtime and praying for a miracle."*
~ *Unknown*

# CONTENTS

| | |
|---|---|
| Introduction | vii |
| 1. Take Your Seat at the Table | 1 |
| 2. Managing Expectations | 31 |
| 3. Bullying | 45 |
| 4. My My My Poker Face | 61 |
| 5. Social Awareness | 76 |
| 6. Reinforcement for Bad Behavior | 81 |
| 7. Recovery | 84 |
| 8. Fire the Warning Shot | 92 |
| 9. The Showdown | 97 |
| 10. Table Talk | 104 |
| 11. The Family Pot | 120 |
| 12. Learned Helplessness | 127 |
| 13. All-Powerful Children | 135 |
| 14. Passive/Aggressive Players | 139 |
| 15. #SorryNotSorry | 145 |
| 16. You Are Not Their Friend | 148 |
| 17. The Need to Be Unique | 153 |
| 18. Hit Me | 156 |
| 19. The Know-It-All | 161 |
| 20. Enabling | 165 |
| 21. Consistency Is Key | 168 |
| 22. Dealing with a Bad Hand | 171 |
| 23. Follow Through | 174 |
| 24. All in the Details | 177 |
| 25. Clear Communications | 181 |
| 26. Nag, Nag, Nag | 183 |
| 27. No Work, No Pay | 186 |
| 28. Validating Language | 188 |
| 29. Anger, or Is It | 191 |
| 30. Contribution to the Pot | 195 |
| 31. Inevitability of Losing | 197 |

| | |
|---|---|
| 32. Selective Sharing | 200 |
| 33. Projection | 203 |
| 34. Trauma Response | 206 |
| 35. Conclusion | 209 |
| Epilogue | 211 |

# INTRODUCTION

Father's Day 2015 offered a unique opportunity for my father when he participated in the Super Seniors Texas Hold'em World Series of Poker in Las Vegas, Nevada. A thoughtful Christmas gift—a $1,000 entry fee—from his family set the stage for an exciting challenge. Competing against 4,194 entrants, he finished in 503rd place, just shy of the 423rd position needed to win some serious prize money, with the top prize nearing $263,000. Despite not winning, the experience became a cherished family memory.

In his final play, my father confidently pushed all his chips to the center with a pair of Sevens—Pocket Sevens—clutched in his hand. This bold move saw him locked in a heads-up duel, facing just one opponent. His adversary responded by calling the "all-in" with a starting hand known affectionately in poker circles as "big slick"—an Ace and King unsuited, ranking as the eighth strongest possible opening duo in the game. The drama heightened with the reveal of the flop and turn: first a King, and then, devastatingly, another King. In the nativity story, the appearance of three kings heralds joy and celebration, but in the world of poker, they spelled the end of my father's journey in the Super Seniors World Series of Poker. This trio

viii    INTRODUCTION

of kings effectively dethroned his pocket Sevens, concluding his adventurous stint in the tournament.

My parents are avid participants in a weekly poker league that meets every Wednesday evening for two sessions, one at 6:30 PM and another at 9:30 PM. After eight weeks of spirited play, the top 24 players with the most accumulated points are invited to a special tournament with prize money on the line. Success in this league is measured by *consistency*; the most accomplished players consistently perform well, securing their place among the elite top 24 and a chance to compete for the financial rewards.

Poker has stitched itself into the very fabric of our family's existence. What started as a beloved pastime with my grandparents has transformed into a tradition I now cherish with my neighbors and fellow moms (and yes, we've got our very own mom poker league— stay tuned for more tales from that front). As a youngster, I remember bubbling with anticipation, peering over the table at my parents, grandparents, and older siblings, counting the days until I could claim my own seat at the adult table. In those early days, our family games were quaint—nickels, dimes, and quarters clinking into personal margarine tubs as makeshift banks. As time passed, we upped the ante to the more intricate, high-stakes maneuvers of Texas Hold'em.

At our table, poker etiquette was the unspoken rule of law. Age cut no ice here; the game demanded serious chops. Mastery of the game was expected, no matter if you were green behind the ears or a seasoned hand. Earning a seat at the poker table was a privilege laden with expectations: you *needed* to be well-versed in this game to keep your seat at the table.

After all of us siblings had moved out, my parents transformed their living room into a dedicated poker room, the centerpiece being a beautifully crafted poker table with a plush tan velvet surface and elegant silver-colored cup holders, easily the most luxurious item in their home. In recent years, we've added a new tradition to our family gatherings: a winner-takes-all poker tournament. We had a trophy made, one that carries the prestige of having the winner's name engraved on it. Winning this trophy is considered the highest honor in our family, a testament to skill and familial pride that intensifies our bonds during these spirited reunions.

For many, poker might simply be a game—a lucrative one for those who master it. In our family, though, it has always been much more. It provided rare moments of togetherness for a family characterized by diverse personalities and varied interests. Poker offered us a common language, a means of connection where everyone could engage equally, regardless of our differences.

Now that I'm a parent myself, I'm passing down this treasured family tradition. There's a secret thrill in watching my sixth grader slap down a full house or casually toss out terms like "burn and turn." It's about more than just teaching them the game; it's about passing on a slice of generational nostalgia, a cherished ritual that has stitched our family together through the years. Watching my children master the game, I see more than just strategy unfolding; I see a legacy continuing, one hand at a time.

I've been lucky to find a group of moms who embraced my enthusiasm for poker, leading to the creation of our Wahoo Women's Poker League. It's been a delightful twist of fate, although not without its challenges—these moms are competitive and remarkably quick learners! They've been consistently lightening my wallet, winning my $20 buy-ins almost every time we meet to play. It's all in good fun, but boy, do they keep me on my toes!

Despite these playful losses, there's a profound joy and deep sense of pride in sharing this part of my heritage. Poker, once just a simple game from my childhood, now holds immense significance in my life. It's become a bond I cherish not only with my family but also with a wonderful group of friends. It's more than just a game; it's a tradition that enriches our relationships and brings us closer together, offering a sense of community and connection that feels especially valuable in today's world.

x   INTRODUCTION

## PARENTING VS. POKER

As an adult, and particularly as a parent, reflecting on the nuances of poker has revealed to me just how much it parallels the art of parenting. Indeed, both realms share a foundation in risk and reward, strategy, and the unpredictable nature of outcomes. At its core, deciding to start a family might be one of life's most significant gambles. Like a high-stakes poker game, parenting is all about making pivotal decisions amidst uncertainty, sizing up risks, and tweaking strategies as the family dynamics shuffle and change. The stakes? Sky-high. But the rewards? They're the emotional jackpot, far outstripping any pile of chips on a poker table.

Just as in poker, where a range of playing styles can lead to success or failure, there is no one-size-fits-all approach to parenting. Each parent, like each poker player, brings their unique style to the table—some may be conservative, others liberal, some strategic, and others more intuitive.

What's truly intriguing about both poker and parenting is the lack of a guaranteed winning formula. Unlike many games where specific strategies or moves can boost your chances of victory, poker and parenting don't follow a straight path to success. Various choices, strategies, and styles can lead to triumph, whether it's nurturing a well-adjusted child or sweeping a high-stakes game. This variability and the essential need for adaptability highlight the complexity and richness of both endeavors. It underscores that real success often hinges on how effectively you can adapt and respond to the ever-changing dynamics at play.

In poker, even the most skilled players face the fundamental uncertainty of the game: the *unpredictability* of the cards they'll receive. A player might be dealt a strong hand, yet victory isn't guaranteed, as the outcome depends on a complex interplay of strategy, other players' actions, and luck. Similarly, parenting is filled with uncertainties and risks. Despite best intentions and seemingly effective strategies, outcomes can still be unexpected. This aspect of both poker and parenting can be challenging and humbling, underscoring a shared truth: *success is never guaranteed,* no matter the quality of the "hand" you start with or the decisions you make along the way.

In parenting, like in poker, you can do everything "right"— providing love, setting boundaries, teaching values—and still face moments where things don't go as planned. Every parent has those tough days where, despite their best efforts, things just don't go their way, much like a poker player who plays a perfect game yet still comes up short. This reality teaches both poker players and parents the importance of resilience, adaptability, and the humility to accept and learn from less-than-ideal outcomes.

In poker, understanding the basics—how to bet, fold, call, or raise —is just the start. Players must continually adapt to the unpredictable dynamics of each round, the varied strategies of opponents, and the randomness of the cards dealt. This ongoing uncertainty requires flexibility and resilience.

Parenting mirrors this experience. While parents might know the basic "rules" or principles of raising children—providing love, setting boundaries, teaching values—the real challenge lies in applying these amidst the unpredictability of daily life. Each child's unique personality and needs mean strategies that motivate or discipline one child might not work for another. Like poker players who adjust their strategies based on the hand they're dealt and their opponents' moves, parents learn to tailor their approaches to each child's individuality.

This duality of feeling like an expert and a novice all at once captures the paradox of parenting. It's an experience steeped in simultaneous confidence and doubt, a familiar terrain for parents everywhere. Through a mix of trial and error, parents come to realize that there's no universal playbook; effective parenting demands a strategy that shifts and grows with the unique temperament and needs of each child. Though this journey is riddled with uncertainties, it's these very challenges that enrich the parenting adventure, deepening understanding and strengthening family ties.

xii  INTRODUCTION

## WHAT TO EXPECT?

I want to begin by setting clear expectations: the content that follows is simply information, crafted to be both useful and engaging. Think of it as a helpful companion or a manual—essentially, a "Poker Player's Guide to Parenting." My goal with this book is to offer insights and strategies that might not only make the complex game of parenting more manageable but also more enjoyable. By drawing parallels between the strategic nuances of poker and the day-to-day challenges of parenting, I aim to provide you with tools that can enhance the quality of the time you spend with your children. Whether you are a seasoned parent or just starting your journey, I hope that this guide serves as a supportive resource that enriches your family life, making every moment count with wisdom, humor, and a touch of card-playing cunning.

Before I became a parent, my view on parenting was worlds apart from where I stand now. Back in my life B.C. (Before Children), I enjoyed the bliss of ample time and the freedom to concoct theories about parenting. Armed with this leisure, I confidently believed I had the golden answers that all parents were searching for. I thought parenting was a straightforward game, governed by a neat set of rules. Looking back, I can't help but chuckle at my naivety.

Now, with three children in the mix, my grasp of parenting has shifted dramatically. I've learned firsthand that parenting is a wildly complex and nuanced endeavor. The challenges and surprises it throws at you can't be neatly dodged with a cookie-cutter set of rules. This journey has completely transformed my views and strategies, enriching my understanding in ways I could never have imagined in those serene, pre-parenting days.

Reflecting on my time as a Child and Family Therapist before I had children, I met parents who were openly skeptical of my advice, wondering how someone without children could really get the full picture of their parenting struggles. I tried not to take it personally, aiming to keep my cool and stay empathetic, but they had a point.

How could I truly grasp the rollercoaster of parenting without riding it myself?

Now, as a parent, I see things from a new perspective. I realize how I might have unintentionally made some parents feel misunderstood or even judged. For this, I offer my sincere apologies. Parenting is an intensely personal journey, and what works for one family may not work for another. My earlier views, while packed with good intentions, missed those priceless insights that only come from diving headfirst into the parenting pool.

Looking back, I understand why a parent might be hesitant to take advice from someone who hasn't faced the day-to-day realities of raising a child. Now, I might find it challenging myself to fully embrace guidance from a younger, childless therapist, despite their expertise and good intentions. This realization has humbled me and enriched my professional practice, reminding me that personal experience often provides a deeper understanding that complements academic knowledge and professional training.

After our first child arrived, my involvement with this project unsurprisingly took a backseat, and it stayed parked there for quite some time. Amid the delightful chaos of parenting, I not only forgot about the project I had once been so eager to dive into but also seemed to misplace many of the therapeutic strategies I was once adept at teaching others. My brain seemed to switch gears completely, adjusting to the all-consuming world of parenting.

Whether you call it pregnancy brain, baby brain, or toddler brain, this mental juggling act was no small feat. It felt like my cognitive processes were more focused on nursery rhymes than neural pathways! Looking back, I'm half-amazed, half-amused that my children have managed to flourish given the comedy of errors that is new parenthood.

As we approach the first chapter of this journey, I feel both blessed and exhilarated to share these insights with you. This book has been a labor of love, a project born from both professional understanding and personal experience. Delving back into these concepts,

xiv  INTRODUCTION

reflecting on my own adventures in parenting, and drawing parallels to the strategic nuances of poker has been an enriching process. I've unearthed cherished memories and gathered valuable lessons that I am eager to pass along to you. Whether you're a poker enthusiast, a seasoned parent, or someone just starting out on the parenting path, I hope you find as much value in reading this book as I have had in writing it. Here's to the shared strategies, laughter, and learning that lie ahead. Let's begin this adventure together.

# CHAPTER 1

## TAKE YOUR SEAT AT THE TABLE

Navigating the world of casinos can be incredibly intimidating, especially when it comes to finding a seat at a poker table. While I've never actually played poker in a casino myself, the thought alone brings up a myriad of questions. Can you simply take any available seat, or is there a waiting list you need to join? Should you wait for the current game to end, or is it okay to slide in mid-shuffle and pretend you know what's going on? What about the buy-in—how much do you need to bring to the table? And then there are the unspoken rules and etiquette that seasoned players seem to know instinctively.

---

*Pro tip:* *If everyone at the table stops talking and stares when you sit down, you might want to reconsider your life choices—or at least your seat.*

---

Now, wouldn't it be nice if casinos handed out a little brochure titled "Poker for Dummies: How Not to Embarrass Yourself in Front of Strangers"? But alas, no such luck. This lack of guidance can make the experience even more daunting. Perhaps this uncertainty is what led me to start my own poker club—a friendlier, less intimidating environment where I could control the snacks and ensure no one was taking the game too seriously. In our club, we learn the ropes together, share our questionable knowledge, and enjoy the game without the pressure of a high-stakes casino atmosphere.

Every new parent can relate to the intimidation and anxiety that come with stepping into the uncharted territory of parenthood for the first time. Much like finding a spot at a poker table, becoming a parent brings a flood of uncertainties and questions. I often hear that no one is ever truly ready for the experience of becoming a parent. Just when you think you've got it figured out, life throws you a curveball—or, in poker terms, deals you a Seven-Deuce off-suit, and you have to make the best of it.

With this monumental change comes a seemingly endless array of questions: What should I expect? How do I handle different situations? What's the best way to care for a newborn? How do I stop the baby from crying? What's the best way to burp them without getting spit-up all over my favorite shirt? Is it normal for me to be this exhausted? (Spoiler: Yes, yes, it is.)

Before a poker player can join a tournament, they must decide whether or not to "buy in." This buy-in represents a fixed monetary investment with the hope of a return, though there are no guarantees. If successful, the investment yields a higher monetary return. For instance, in a $50 buy-in tournament with 50 players and a winner-takes-all format, the winner would take home $2,500. It's a gamble, as the player doesn't know if their $50 investment will be lost or if it will result in a significant payout.

Parenthood is pretty much the same thing, only the stakes are a lot higher, and the payout? Immeasurable! When you decide to become a parent, you're making an investment of time, energy, and every last ounce of your patience. You don't know what the future holds—whether you'll raise the next Einstein or someone who thinks ketchup is a root vegetable—but you dive in anyway, because the potential for joy, fulfillment, and a well-earned legacy is worth the gamble.

Within the family context, "buying-in" as a parent represents the profound investment you make in your children. This commitment goes far beyond the money; it encompasses the emotional and physical energy you and your partner devote to being the absolute best parents you can be. This type of investment, made early in your children's lives, will yield the highest return—happy, healthy children who grow into well-adjusted teens and young adults. And while it is a massive gamble, the potential reward makes it well-worth every sleepless night and every round of the never-ending "Why?" game.

As you may have gathered from the biblical reference in the introduction, my parents are devout Catholics. They made sure to send me and my four siblings to Catholic high school. They believed that a Catholic education was a worthwhile investment, reflecting their values and commitment to our upbringing. While I am no longer a member of the Catholic Church, having joined a Congregational Church instead, it's a family joke that "four out of five isn't bad." Four of the five of us remain practicing Catholics, indicating that my parents' investment was largely successful, despite one divergence.

My husband and I, on the other hand, have different approaches when it comes to investing in our children. He's the creative type—always encouraging the children to express themselves through art, music, and all things messy. He's the kind of dad who will turn a rainy day into an impromptu art class, with paints and crafts everywhere (including the floors and walls, much to my dismay). Me? I'm more about structure, education, and keeping the chaos to a minimum. I'm the one who signs them up for sports practices, reads them bedtime stories, and makes sure they're eating their vegetables (and no, ketchup doesn't count).

We might have different parenting styles, but together, we make it work. It's like we're playing a tag team poker match—he handles the creative bluffs, and I manage the disciplined calls. Between the two of us, we're hoping to hit the jackpot: well-rounded children who can both color inside the lines and think outside the box.

REFLECTION QUESTIONS:

- Think about a time when you had to "buy in" big for your children. What was the outcome? Did you hit the jackpot, or was it more of a learning experience?

- Reflecting on your own childhood, in what ways did your parents invest in you, and how do you think those investments have shaped who you are today? Are there areas where you felt your parents could have been more supportive or involved?

- How do you and your partner balance your different strengths when it comes to raising your children? What lessons have you learned from this dynamic?

THE HAND YOU'RE DEALT

In poker, a game begins with a "hand" being dealt. This hand, a combination of cards given to a player, is used to compete against others with the aim of winning. But here's the catch: your success isn't just about the cards you're holding; it's all about how well you play them. You can't just sit around waiting for the perfect hand to magically appear—life's too short for that, and the poker gods aren't always generous. It's easy to win with a perfect hand, but the real challenge and skill lie in playing well with less-than-ideal cards. This advice translates so well into many aspects of life: *you do the best you can with the hand you've been dealt.* Sometimes, that means playing a mediocre hand like it's the best thing since sliced bread.

As parents, this couldn't be more true. We all dream of the perfect family, with 2.5 children who are always polite, never make a mess, and somehow manage to sleep through the night from day one. But real life? Well, let's just say it deals us all kinds of hands. The measure of happiness and success in parenting isn't about having the ideal circumstances but rather about how we navigate and manage the awful hands we sometimes get.

Take parents of children with major medical conditions, for example. They didn't choose that hand but they play it with a level of strength and grace that's nothing short of inspiring. They're proof that you don't need the perfect hand to win—you just need the right attitude and a whole lot of love. By focusing on love, support, and a healthy dose of resilience, we can create fulfilling and joyful family lives, no matter what cards we've been dealt.

Now, take a moment to think about the circumstances in your life that were beyond your control—the hands you were dealt that you didn't exactly ask for, but you played anyway. Maybe it was a tough childhood, a challenging relationship, or an unexpected career shift. These are your hands in the game of life, and while you don't get to choose your cards, you do get to choose how you play them.

How did you adapt, learn, and grow from those situations? What strengths did you discover within yourself? And how have these experiences shaped you into the person you are today? It's in these challenging hands that we often find our greatest strengths and deepest wisdom. They teach us resilience, patience, and the importance of keeping a cool head under pressure.

## DOWN CARDS

In poker, each player kicks off the hand with two cards dealt face down, known as "down cards." These little secrets are yours and yours alone—no one else at the table has a clue what you're holding.

It's all about strategy, mystery, and, let's be honest, a bit of poker face magic. The thrill of the game lies in what you do with those hidden cards, whether you've got a pair of kings or a couple of deuces.

But here's the thing: life, much like poker, comes with its own set of down cards. Within the family context, your down cards are the unique circumstances and challenges that are specific to you and your loved ones. Just like in poker, these down cards are known only to you and can shape the way you choose to navigate life. Every family has its own deck to deal with, and every individual within that family is holding their own set of cards—some good, some not so good, and some that make you wish you could ask for a re-deal.

Now, in poker, you might keep your down cards close to your chest, flashing a confident grin as you bluff your way through a hand. In life, our down cards often represent the parts of our lives we keep private, the struggles and triumphs that are ours alone to carry. Maybe you share them with a select few, or maybe you keep them hidden, choosing instead to face the world with your best poker face. Either way, these down cards are crucial—they shape the way you play your hand in the game of life.

This whole idea of down cards brings to mind that famous quote by Socrates: "Be kind, for everyone you meet is fighting a hard battle." Just like in poker, where your opponents have no idea what you're holding, in life, we often have no idea what battles others are facing. Those down cards—whether they're positive, negative, or somewhere in between—define how we live, love, and navigate our unique challenges.

Take my close friend, for example. Her down card? The heart-breaking struggle she and her husband face with not being able to carry a baby to full term. It's a deeply personal, painful experience, one that she keeps private, much like a poker player protecting a weak hand. She doesn't share this with the world, not because she's ashamed, but because it's a card she's decided to hold close. It's her way of protecting herself from further emotional pain, her way of maintaining control in a situation that feels overwhelmingly out of control.

In poker, down cards are your hidden strength—or weakness—and how you play them can make all the difference. The same goes for life. Your family's down cards are the stories, the struggles, and the victories that aren't always visible to the outside world. They're the cards you hold tight to your chest, the ones that define your strategy in the game of life.

To make the most of their down cards, parents should first acknowledge and accept these hidden challenges or strengths as a natural part of life. By understanding their unique circumstances, people can make informed decisions, play to their strengths, and mitigate potential weaknesses. Sharing these down cards selectively with trusted individuals can also build support networks and foster deeper connections.

In the end, we all have our down cards—those hidden aspects of our lives we navigate with the best strategy we can muster. They're the challenges we face, the secrets we keep, and the strengths we discover when we least expect them. How you play those cards is up to you, but remember: even a pair of deuces can win the pot if you play them right.

## THE FLOP AND TURN

In poker, the "Flop" is that thrilling moment when the first three community cards are dealt face-up for everyone to see. These are the cards that can either make or break your hand, turning a so-so start into a potential winner or a complete bust. Then comes the "Turn," the fourth card dealt face-up, which can either solidify your strategy or leave you scrambling for a backup plan. It's all part of the game, where every new card brings new possibilities—and new challenges.

In the family game, the Flop represents those universal circumstances we all encounter—things like school, work, and major life events. These are the cards everyone has to work with, but how they impact each family can vary wildly depending on the unique "down cards" that each person is holding. Then comes the Turn, the unexpected developments that add a twist to the story, for better or worse.

Picture this: a parent gets offered a big promotion at work, which sounds like the perfect Turn, right? More money, more prestige, and maybe even a corner office with a view! But here's the catch—the promotion requires the family to relocate to a different state. For the parent, this might feel like hitting the jackpot. But for the children? Well, they might see it as more of a bust, facing the prospect of leaving their friends, their school, and everything familiar behind. Suddenly, that Turn card doesn't look so great to everyone at the table.

Take my father's final hand at the 2015 SSWSOP. The Flop and Turn revealed two kings. For his opponent, it was a dream come true. But for my father? It was more like a nightmare. Those community cards favored his opponent's hand. It's a perfect example of how the same cards can mean very different things to different players.

And isn't that just like parenting? When my husband and I announced to our son and daughter that we were expecting a third child—a boy—our son practically jumped for joy. He was ready to welcome his new little brother with open arms, already dreaming up plans for sibling mischief. But our daughter? Let's just say she wasn't quite as thrilled. To her, this wasn't just a new baby; it was an unwelcome disruption to her perfectly balanced world. The same event, but two totally different reactions.

As parents, it's crucial to remember that each child (and, let's be honest, each adult) reacts differently to the same set of circumstances. What might be a winning hand for one could feel like a losing streak for another. Our job is to recognize those differences and navigate them with empathy, understanding that each family member's perspective is valid, even if it's not what we were hoping for. So how do we handle this delicate balancing act? How can we, as parents, be mindful of both positive and negative responses to the same circumstances in our children?

THE POKER PLAYER'S GUIDE TO PARENTING　9

We can't expect that every change will be met with cheers and high-fives. But we can work to mitigate the negativity by acknowledging their feelings and helping them find the silver linings. It's about showing them that it's okay to feel disappointed or scared, but also encouraging resilience, reminding them that every Turn card has the potential to lead to something great—if we're willing to play it with an open mind.

---

"In poker and parenting, sometimes you've got to play the long game. It's not about winning every hand, but making sure you're still in the game when the final card is dealt."

---

Ultimately, just like in poker, family life is about playing your hand with both individual and community cards in mind. It's about finding a way to balance shared experiences with personal feelings, and supporting each family member through the ups and downs. Because in this game, the real victory comes not from winning every hand, but from staying in the game together, no matter what cards are dealt.

REFLECTION QUESTIONS:

- How can we, as parents, stay mindful of the fact that the same circumstances can elicit both positive and negative responses in our children? What signs help you recognize their unique reactions?

- While we can't always expect positivity, what strategies can we use to help mitigate negative responses—whether it's offering support, reframing the situation, or providing space for them to process emotions?

# LEAHA HAMMER

- How do you balance acknowledging your child's negative feelings without minimizing them, while still encouraging resilience and problem-solving?

- In what ways can you help your child learn that experiencing negative emotions is normal, but how they respond to those emotions is where their strength lies?

## THE RIVER CARD

In poker, the "River Card" is the fifth and final card dealt face-up on the table, the one that has the power to make or break your entire game. It's the card that can turn your pair into a full house or crush your dreams of winning the pot. After the River is dealt, players enter the last round of betting, and this is where the rubber meets the road. The stakes are high, the pressure is on, and everyone has to make some crucial decisions based on all the cards in play.

In the game of life, the River card represents those moments when everything is on the table, and it's time to make a final call. It's that point where you've gathered all the information, assessed the situation, and now you've got to decide what to do next. No more waiting for the perfect card to show up—this is it!

Imagine you're a parent, and your child has been offered a fantastic opportunity to attend a prestigious school in a land far away from home, not quite *Hogwarts*—but close! It's the kind of offer that could open up a world of possibilities for your children's future, but it also means uprooting the entire family, leaving behind a support network, and starting life anew in an unfamiliar place. The River card is on the table, and now you've got to weigh the benefits of this opportunity against the potential challenges it brings.

Much like in poker, making the final decision as a parent is rarely black and white. It involves carefully considering all the factors at play, from financial stability and career prospects to your children's emotional well-being and the family's overall happiness. And let's be real—it's not just about logic and spreadsheets. There's a lot of heart in these decisions, and sometimes, it feels like no matter what you choose, you're going to be leaving something important behind.

But here's where the game gets interesting: even with all the cards on the table, you've still got the power to influence the outcome. Just like a seasoned poker player knows when to bet, fold, or bluff, as a parent, you've got to *trust your instincts*, listen to your heart, and make the best call for your family.

In poker, the River card can be a game-changer. In life, those River moments—whether it's deciding on a big move, a career change, or how to support your child through a tough time—require us to dig deep, think critically, and sometimes take a leap of faith. It's not easy, but by being mindful of both the positive and negative outcomes, validating everyone's feelings, and encouraging resilience, you can navigate these decisions with greater clarity and confidence.

REFLECTION QUESTIONS:

- What key factors does your family typically consider when making significant decisions? Think about elements like financial stability, career opportunities, educational needs, health concerns, or emotional well-being.

- How has each of these factors influenced your decision-making process? Were some weighed more heavily than others?

- Reflect on a recent major decision your family made. How did balancing these considerations shape the final outcome?

Remember, in the end, it's not just about the cards you're dealt, but how you play them. And sometimes, it's the toughest hands that bring out the best in us.

---

"Life's River card: sometimes it's a straight flush, sometimes it's just a flush of emotions. But either way, you've got to make your move."

---

## WIN THE POT

In poker, the goal is simple: *win the pot*. The pot represents the accumulation of poker chips that will be awarded to the player with the best hand. It's the ultimate reward, the thing that keeps everyone around the table focused, strategizing, and daydreaming about the mountains of cash sitting mere inches away from their faces.

But let's take a step back from the poker table and into the world of parenting. What's the equivalent of the pot when it comes to motivating your children? The answer isn't as straightforward as a stack of poker chips. For a poker player, the reward is cold, hard cash (or at least, the promise of it). For children, though, the "pot" can take many different forms, and figuring out what it is might require a bit of detective work on your part.

You've probably heard the phrase, "What makes them tick?" This little saying is all about motivation—what drives someone to take action. And when it comes to children, it's all about finding out what their personal currency is. What form of "payment" will get them to clean their room, finish their homework, or stop launching peas across the dinner table at their baby sister like they're in some kind of vegetable catapult competition?

For some children, their currency is all about praise and positive reinforcement. Compliments, high-fives, and a big ol' "Great job!" can light up their world and motivate them to keep doing whatever it is you're encouraging. Other children might be more interested in tangible rewards—think stickers, toys, or that extra ten minutes of screen time they've been bargaining for. And then there are the children who are all about privileges: staying up a bit later, choosing the family movie, or inviting a friend over for a playdate.

The trick is to figure out what makes your child tick. What's their currency? And once you know that, you can "use it" to your advantage.

It might take some experimentation, but you'll get there. Observe their reactions to different types of rewards, and see what they value most. Do they light up when you praise their efforts, or do they get more excited about earning a new toy? Are they motivated by the idea of having more control over their day, like choosing what's for dinner or planning a weekend activity? Understanding what drives your child will help you tailor your approach to encouragement and motivation, just like a savvy poker player tailors their strategy to the cards they're dealt.

---

"In the poker game of parenting, the pot isn't just money—it's whatever makes your child go, 'Deal me in!'"

---

And here's a little secret: if you're feeling guilty about "bribing" your children to do what you want, you're not alone. But let's call it what it really is: strategic motivation. I once worked as a child therapist and met a parent who was completely appalled by the idea of using bribery to elicit appropriate behavior from their children. To that, I say, why not? Isn't parenting essentially an 18+ year series of bribery and negotiations?

Think about it. Who hasn't promised their child a treat if they just behave for five more minutes in the grocery store? Or offered a special reward for getting through a particularly tough week of school? Let's be real—bribery, when used strategically, is one of the most important and powerful tools in a parent's arsenal. It's not about "tricking" your children; it's about giving them an incentive to do the right thing, just like how a poker player works to win the pot.

So, the next time you find yourself negotiating with your little one, remember that just like in poker, it's all about the strategy. Find their currency, use it wisely, and watch as they work toward that pot.

## FAMILY POT

In the world of poker, there's a phrase you might hear when everything's going smoothly: "The pot's right." This means that each player has put in the correct amount of money, and the dealer can move forward with the game. It's a way of saying that everyone is in, everyone's committed, and the game can continue. There's also something called a "family pot," which happens when every player decides to stay in the game, contributing their share and remaining engaged in the round. It's a rare and exciting moment when everyone's on the same page.

Now, let's swap the poker table for the kitchen table. In the context of family life, the idea of a "family pot" can be a powerful metaphor for how we all contribute to the collective good of the household. Just like poker players put their chips in the pot to keep the game going, each member of the family puts in their share—whether it's time, effort, or just a little extra patience—to ensure the family runs smoothly.

Of course, expecting my young children to contribute as much as my spouse or myself is about as likely as winning a poker game with a Seven-Deuce off-suit. But that doesn't mean they get a free pass. Just because they're not tossing in stacks of chips doesn't mean they can't contribute to the family pot in meaningful ways. Their contributions should be appropriate for their age, ability, and level of maturity. For example, a child might contribute by helping with small chores, showing kindness, or simply being responsible for their own belongings.

Think of it this way: just as a poker hand can't move forward until each player who has decided to call puts in their chips, a family can't function effectively without everyone pitching in. It doesn't have to be equal—it just has to be fair. The collective effort ensures that the family functions smoothly and that everyone feels valued and responsible.

In our household, my spouse and I handle the big-ticket items: financial stability, guidance, and emotional support. We're the ones keeping the lights on and making sure there's food on the table. But our older children? They've got their own responsibilities, like helping with household tasks or looking after their younger siblings. And the younger ones? Well, they're learning the ropes—being responsible for their actions, helping with simple chores, and even contributing emotionally with their love and affection.

It's a delicate balance, though. Just like in poker, where every player's contribution matters, in a family, everyone's input is crucial. But fairness is key. How do we ensure that the expectations we place on our children are fair, especially when there's a significant age gap between the oldest and youngest? It's like making sure the pot is right —everyone contributes what they can, based on their ability, and the game (or in this case, the family) moves forward.

- How do you contribute to your family?
- How does your spouse chip in?
- What about your children?
- How do you handle the tricky issue of fairness, especially when your older children might feel like they're doing more than their younger siblings?

The key is to make sure that everyone feels like they're part of the game, that their contributions—no matter how small—are valued and important. When everyone's putting into the family pot, you'll find that not only does the household run more smoothly, but everyone also feels more connected, responsible, and appreciated.

Just like in poker, where the size of the pot can vary depending on the players' bets, the "currency" or reward that each child receives is dependent on their contribution to the family. So when your 12-year-old starts grumbling about being stuck with dish duty while their 6-year-old sibling gets off easy, it's a great opportunity to remind them that their effort is being recognized—and yes, they're getting "bribed" for it. Whatever their currency is, whether it's extra screen time, a special treat, or staying up a little later, they'll appreciate it more when they understand that their reward is higher because their contribution is bigger. It's all about fair play, and just like in poker, the bigger the bet, the bigger the potential reward.

## FOLD, CALL, OR BET

In poker, once you've been dealt your two down cards, the game begins with a crucial decision: do you *fold, call*, or *bet*? Folding means you're bowing out—you don't think your hand has what it takes to win, so you cut your losses and move on to the next round. Calling or betting, on the other hand, means you're in. You've got at least some confidence in those cards, and you're willing to invest a bit more to see where they take you. Folding might suggest caution, a calculated retreat, while calling or betting signals that you're ready to take a chance, even if it's just a small one.

Now, let's bring this back to the high-stakes game of parenting. Every day, we're dealt situations where we have to decide: do we engage, or do we let it go? Is this battle worth fighting, or is it better to fold and save our energy for something more important down the line?

Take, for instance, the Great Sandal Standoff of when my oldest son was two years old. We had just bought him new sandals for the summer, thinking they'd be perfect for the warmer weather. They were cooler, more comfortable—what's not to love, right? Well, apparently, plenty. Our son wasn't ready to part with his beloved Lightning McQueen Velcro sneakers. Those sneakers were his comfort zone, his go-to, and no amount of coaxing could convince him otherwise (just like Lightning McQueen, well played!). So, what did we do? We folded. We decided it wasn't worth the battle to insist on the new sandals. Let the child wear his sneakers—we'll save our energy for something bigger.

This approach applies to so many parenting scenarios. As parents, we're constantly making decisions about which battles to engage in and which to let go. Do we fight every fight, or do we pick our battles wisely? For example, if your child refuses to eat broccoli but happily munches on carrots and green beans, maybe you fold on the broccoli. After all, they're still getting their veggies, right? Or if your child insists on wearing a tutu over their jeans to school, do you really want to argue about it? Sometimes, folding means recognizing that a little self-expression is more important than perfectly matching outfits.

The key is to prioritize what truly matters for your child's well-being and development. Engaging in every battle is a recipe for exhaustion—for both you and your child. It can lead to unnecessary stress and conflict, turning your home into a constant battleground. But by strategically choosing which issues to address, you can create a more positive and cooperative family dynamic. By folding on the less critical issues, you save your energy for the ones that really matter, fostering a more harmonious and supportive environment for everyone.

REFLECTION QUESTIONS:

- Can you recall a time when you had to "fold" as a parent —letting go of a battle that just wasn't worth the stress? What was the outcome, and how did it affect your perspective moving forward?

- What's an example of a situation where you decided to "call" or "bet"—standing your ground because the issue truly mattered? How did that decision impact your family dynamic?

- How do you determine which battles are worth fighting and which ones are better left alone for the sake of overall harmony?

Remember, in both poker and parenting, the decisions you make are rarely black and white. It's all about strategy, intuition, and sometimes just going with your gut. The real art lies in knowing which hands to play and which to fold, keeping the bigger picture in mind.

By folding on the small stuff, you reserve your strength for the big stuff, the issues that really shape your child's growth and your family's well-being. And when you do decide to call or bet, you'll do so with the confidence that it's truly worth it.

## COMPROMISE

In poker, once you've been dealt your hand, you might find yourself in a sticky spot. You don't want to fold, but staying in the game feels a little too risky. Unfortunately, there's no way to split the difference in poker. It's all or nothing—you're either in or you're out. But when it comes to parenting, that's where the beauty of compromise comes in. The ability to find a middle ground, as long as it doesn't *compromise* safety or core values, is one of the most powerful tools in a parent's arsenal.

Compromise allows for a balanced approach where both parties feel heard and respected. It's about creating a space where your child can express their opinions without automatically agreeing to everything. You don't want a child who nods along like a bobblehead, never feeling comfortable enough to voice their thoughts. Expressing an opinion doesn't mean the child will always get what they want, but it does mean their voice is heard and valued.

Let's say your child wants to stay up an extra hour past bedtime. You could shut it down with a flat "no" or cave in completely, but there's a sweet spot in between. Maybe you compromise by allowing an extra 15 minutes for a special occasion. This way, your child feels their request was considered, but the compromise still respects the importance of a consistent bedtime. It's like giving them a small taste of victory without handing over the whole pot.

When children are encouraged to express their opinions and sometimes reach a compromise, they learn a valuable life skill: *how to cope with disappointment*. They understand that while they may not always get what they want, their thoughts and feelings are acknowledged. This approach reduces anxiety and builds better communication between parent and child. When children feel heard, they're more likely to be open and honest in the future. They may not always get their way, but they won't be reluctant to communicate with you or feel the need to withhold their thoughts. This openness lays the groundwork for a strong, respectful, and understanding parent-child relationship.

Now, let's clear up a common misconception: compromising or giving your child occasional power doesn't mean you're losing yours. In fact, it does the exact opposite. As parents, our goal is to nurture independent thinkers, and one of the best ways to do that is by encouraging communication and compromise. Ultimately, parents have the final say, but we also have the opportunity to recognize when our child makes a valid point or expresses their opinion respectfully. This approach doesn't diminish parental power; instead, it strengthens the parent-child relationship and fosters a sense of mutual respect. The simple act of compromise can significantly boost a child's confidence and sense of autonomy.

*"When you compromise with your children, you're not folding—you're playing a smarter hand."*

Knowing when to compromise is an essential skill in both parenting and life. Just as in poker, where knowing when to fold can be a smart strategy, understanding when to give your child a bit of control can be equally wise. It shows that you respect their growing independence and trust their judgment, fostering a positive and empowering environment.

So, the next time you find yourself in a standoff with your child, remember that compromise isn't a sign of weakness. It's a strategic move that can lead to stronger relationships and a more harmonious household. In the end, it's about finding that balance where everyone feels valued and respected, and where your child learns that sometimes, meeting in the middle is the best way to win the game.

## KNOW WHEN NOT TO FOLD

In poker, folding every hand is a surefire way to lose. If you're constantly bowing out, never taking a stand, you might as well hand your chips over to the other players and call it a night. The same principle applies to parenting. If you find yourself compromising too frequently, letting your child feel like they're running the show, you're setting yourself up for a loss—not just in the moment, but in the long-term dynamics of your household.

Imagine what would happen if I folded to my children every time a conflict arose. Pretty soon, I'd be living in a house where the bedtime routine is a distant memory, vegetables are an endangered species, and the Wi-Fi password is held hostage by a six-year-old negotiator. Sure, it might keep the peace in the short term, but in the long run? You'd end up with a household where the children are running the table, and you're left wondering how you got dealt such a lousy hand.

In poker, the key to success is knowing which hands to play and which to fold. You've got to maintain a strategic balance, picking your battles wisely to maximize your chances of winning. And guess what? Parenting isn't all that different. It's essential to strike that delicate balance between being firm and being flexible. Some situations demand that you stand your ground, assert your authority, and set clear boundaries. In other scenarios, compromise and negotiation are the best moves, showing your child the importance of give-and-take in relationships.

This balancing act is crucial. By selectively choosing when to stand firm and when to bend, you can maintain your authority while fostering a respectful and cooperative family environment. It's like being a skilled poker player who knows that not every hand can be a winner, but that strategic losses are sometimes necessary for long-term success. You don't need to fight every battle, but you do need to know when and where to draw the line.

Take bedtime, for example. If your child wants to stay up late every night, and you constantly give in, you're essentially folding every time. But if you occasionally compromise with a "five more minutes" on a special night, while sticking to a firm bedtime on most nights, you're showing that you're willing to be flexible—but not a pushover. Your child learns that while their opinions matter, there are still rules in place that need to be followed.

Effective parenting, much like effective poker playing, involves understanding the dynamics at play, recognizing the stakes, and making informed decisions that balance short-term actions with long-term goals. It requires a strategic mindset, patience, and the ability to read the situation accurately, adapting your approach as necessary to maintain both authority and harmony within the family.

So, the next time you're faced with a standoff over screen time, dessert, or whether or not they can wear pajamas to school, remember: not every situation calls for a fold. Sometimes, standing firm is the best way to ensure long-term respect and balance within your household.

---

"In poker and parenting, folding is an option—but knowing when not to fold? That's where the real game is won."

---

In essence, being a parent is all about mastering the art of strategic compromise while knowing when it's time to hold your ground. It's not always easy, but then again, neither is poker. But with a little patience, a lot of love, and a well-timed poker face, you'll keep the chips stacked in your favor and the family dynamics right where they need to be.

## THE LIMP-IN

In poker, when a player "limps-in," they're calling the minimum bet, choosing not to raise the stakes. It's a move that doesn't necessarily scream weakness, but it often suggests a lack of confidence or uncertainty about the strength of their position. You're in the game, but you're not all in. You're playing it safe, maybe waiting to see how the cards (or the other players) fall before making a bigger move.

Sound familiar? It should, because this analogy resonates deeply with parenting. As parents, we frequently question our decisions, wondering, "Am I doing the right thing?" This uncertainty can stem from the immense responsibility we feel towards our children and the desire to make the best choices for their well-being and future. Just like a poker player who limps-in, parents may find themselves taking a cautious approach, unsure of the potential outcomes of their actions.

In poker, a player who limps-in might be testing the waters, gathering information, and observing how others at the table respond before committing to a more decisive move. It's a cautious, sometimes tentative step forward, and parenting can feel the same way. You're not quite ready to go all in because, let's be honest, raising children can feel like the highest-stakes game there is. So, you proceed with caution, seeking more information and reassurance before making those big, impactful decisions that shape your family's future.

But here's the thing: uncertainty is a natural part of the parenting journey. Just like poker, parenting is an ever-evolving game that requires adaptability, patience, and a willingness to learn from experience. Embracing that uncertainty—rather than letting it paralyze you—can lead to growth and better decision-making over time. Just as a poker player gains confidence through practice and experience, parents, too, can build confidence by acknowledging their doubts, seeking guidance when needed, and learning from each step they take in their parenting journey.

Take my own experience, for example. When my oldest son was five, I faced a significant parenting dilemma. Both my husband and I had been deeply involved in athletics throughout our lives, so naturally, I wanted to offer our son the opportunity to participate in various sports. Visions of basketball and football practices danced in my head. But to my surprise, he showed absolutely no interest in joining any athletic activities. Zero. Zilch. Nada.

This left me grappling with uncertainty and questioning my approach. Should I push him into something I loved, or let him find his own path? I was limping in, unsure of the right move. So, like any parent searching for answers, I reached out to others. "Is your child resisting athletic participation?" I asked, hoping for a lifeline. The responses were mostly unanimous: their children loved playing basketball, football or whatever sport they were involved in. Great, just what I needed—more confusion. I then asked these parents if they would require their child to participate in sports even if the child showed no interest. As expected, the feedback was mixed.

This led me to a critical question: by forcing my son to participate in sports, was I doing the right thing? Or should I respect his desire to abstain from athletic activities and allow him to make his own decision? The struggle was real. On one hand, I valued my son's opinion and wanted to respect his feelings. On the other hand, I suspected that his reluctance stemmed from a lack of prior experience and an anxiety about the unknown. He had no basis for his disinterest other than the fact that he had never tried it before.

So, what's a parent to do? After much deliberation, I decided to take a calculated risk. We registered him for basketball, encouraging him to give it a shot. I tried to keep it low-pressure, framing it as an opportunity to try something new rather than a commitment to a lifetime of athletic glory.

And you know what? I'm happy to report that he ended up really enjoying it. The reluctant participant turned into an enthusiastic player, and I was left wondering why I'd ever worried in the first place. This experience taught me a valuable lesson about balancing my child's expressed desires with my parental intuition about what's best for him. Sometimes, encouraging a child to step out of their comfort zone can lead to wonderful new experiences and personal growth.

"Sometimes the best hands in parenting are the ones you almost folded on."

Parenting, much like poker, involves making decisions amidst uncertainty. It requires weighing various factors, considering the potential outcomes, and sometimes taking calculated risks. Just as a poker player gains confidence through experience, parents can build confidence by thoughtfully navigating these dilemmas, learning from each situation, and ultimately guiding their children toward opportunities that can enrich their lives.

So, the next time you find yourself questioning whether to push or pull back, remember the limp-in. It's okay to be uncertain, to gather your information and hedge your bets. But sometimes, a little

THE POKER PLAYER'S GUIDE TO PARENTING    25

push—whether it's into a basketball game or a new experience—can lead to something wonderful. And who knows? You might just find that your child, like mine, ends up running full-speed ahead into something they never knew they'd love.

---

"Sometimes you've just got to trust your gut, play the hand, and see where it takes you."

---

- What parental decisions have you made or avoided due to a lack of confidence in "doing the right thing?"
- How did you eventually come to a decision, and was it ultimately the right choice for your family?

## GOING "ALL IN"

I often recall a quote my father used to say: "You can't always wait for pocket Aces to come along." This nugget of wisdom has stuck with me over the years, reminding me that while some decisions are straightforward and obvious, others require a leap of faith and are far more challenging. It's like poker—if you're dealt a Seven and Jack, deciding to play might feel like a gamble, unlike the no-brainer decision to play pocket Aces. (For those who don't speak poker, pocket Aces are the best starting hand, while a Seven and Jack? Well, let's just say it's not a slam dunk

Back when we had our first child, my husband and I were living in Seattle. We both had decent jobs, but we were far from family, living in an apartment, and couldn't foresee affording a home in the neighborhood we desired. We were at a crossroads, facing a tough decision: Should we stay in Seattle, where we had built our lives, or should we move back to Nebraska, where we had family support and a potentially lower cost of living? This decision wasn't as easy as playing pocket Aces; it was more like making a call with that risky 7 and Jack, uncertain of what the future might hold.

Ultimately, we decided to take the leap and move back to Nebraska. It was a gamble, filled with uncertainty about our future jobs, our living situation, and whether or not we'd regret leaving the city we'd grown to love. But here's the kicker: the risk paid off. We found good jobs, a lovely home, and the support of family just around the corner. It wasn't an instant jackpot, but it was a win. This experience highlighted that sometimes, even when the decision isn't obvious or easy, taking a calculated risk can lead to positive outcomes.

---

"Sometimes the biggest wins come from taking a chance on the hands that seem the least promising."

---

In poker, starting with seemingly weak cards—like that 7 and Jack—might seem depressing. But if the community cards—the flop—reveal an 8, 9, and 10, those weak starting cards suddenly form a powerful hand called a straight. Similarly, in parenting, what may seem like challenging or unclear situations can develop into something wonderful with the right circumstances. It's about seeing the potential in what you've been dealt and trusting that sometimes, the best outcomes come from the most uncertain beginnings.

To be all-in in poker means that a player has committed all of their chips to the pot, putting everything on the line in one decisive move. It's the ultimate act of commitment, a bold statement that you're ready to see this through to the end. This type of commitment is strikingly reminiscent of the dedication we make to our children every single day. Whether we're having good days or bad days, whether we're feeling like super parents or just barely holding it together, our commitment to our children remains unwavering. We give it our all, consistently and wholeheartedly.

In poker, going all-in can be a move made with great confidence, a strategic play that demonstrates strength and assurance. Alternatively, it can be a last-ditch effort to stay in the game, a desperate move when there are no other options left. Both scenarios mirror the spectrum of parenting experiences. There are moments when we approach parenting with certainty and clear direction, knowing exactly what needs to be done. We feel like we've got the winning hand, and we're playing it with confidence.

But then there are those other times. You know the ones I'm talking about—the days when you feel like you're barely hanging on, doing whatever it takes just to keep moving forward. It's in these moments that going all-in feels more like a necessity than a choice. You might be exhausted, frustrated, or just plain out of ideas, but you dig deep, push through, and commit everything you've got because, well, that's what parenting demands.

Ultimately, going all-in is about commitment, whether it's the confident, strategic kind or the desperate, "I'll do whatever it takes" kind. It's about showing up, being present, and giving your best, no matter what cards you've been dealt. Because in the game of parenting, the stakes are always high, but the potential rewards? Beyond measure.

---

"In poker and parenting, the biggest risks can yield the greatest rewards—but you've got to be willing to go all-in."

---

So, here's to the moments when we take a chance on a less-than-perfect hand, and to the days when we find ourselves all-in, whether we're ready for it or not. It's all part of the game, and the best we can do is play with heart, hope, and a little bit of humor along the way.

## KEY LESSONS

In both poker and parenting, success depends on navigating uncertainties, making strategic moves, and balancing risks with potential rewards. The skills developed in one can often be applied to the other, highlighting the unexpected parallels between these two seemingly different worlds.

### Key Learnings

- **Intimidation and Anxiety:** Embrace the discomfort of new experiences. Start today by seeking out resources, asking for advice, and reminding yourself that it's okay to not have all the answers.

- **Buy-In:** In poker, this is purely a monetary investment; in parenting, it's the profound investment of time, money, energy, and emotional resources in raising children. Recognize the value of your investment in parenting. Dedicate specific time each day to focus on your child, ensuring that your efforts are meaningful and impactful.

- **The Hand You're Dealt:** Success in both poker and parenting depends on how well you play your cards – making the most of your unique family circumstances. Make the most of your unique circumstances. Identify one area where you can improve or adapt your approach to better suit your family's needs.

- **Down Cards:** These represent the unique, often private challenges each family faces. Challenges that are known only to you and key members of your family, keeping these close to the chest can, and should be, part of your strategy. Acknowledge your family's private challenges. Develop a strategy to address these issues quietly and effectively, ensuring they don't undermine your family dynamics.

- **The Flop and Turn:** These shared experiences can impact each family member differently, requiring sensitive handling by parents. Practice active listening today to better support each family member's individual reactions.

- **The River Card:** This represents the culmination of circumstances where final decisions must be made. Prepare for crucial decisions by weighing all available information. When faced with a major decision, consider all perspectives and potential outcomes before making a final choice.

- **Win the Pot:** Identify what motivates your child and use it to encourage positive behavior. Implement a small reward system to reinforce good habits and actions. In the words of Gordon Gekko: "Bribery is good," I'm paraphrasing.

- **Family Pot:** Ensure everyone in the family contributes appropriately. Assign age-appropriate tasks to each family member to foster a sense of responsibility and teamwork.

- **Fold, Call, or Bet:** Choose your battles wisely. Decide today which minor issues you can let go of to focus on more important matters.

- **Compromise:** Finding middle ground while maintaining core value is crucial. Practice negotiating a solution that respects both your perspective and your child's wishes.

- **Know When NOT to Fold:** Maintain authority by standing firm on essential issues. Identify your non-negotiables and ensure they are clearly communicated and consistently enforced.

- **The Limp-In:** Address parental uncertainty by seeking guidance and trusting your instincts. Take a moment today to reflect on a recent decision, affirming your capability as a parent.

- **Going All In:** Fully commit to things that are important to you, even when the outcome is uncertain. Dedicate yourself to being present and engaged, trusting that your efforts will lead to positive outcomes.

# CHAPTER 2

## MANAGING EXPECTATIONS

In poker, a "bad beat" occurs when a player loses a hand they were certain they would win. You think you've got the game in the bag, only to have the rug pulled out from under you at the last second. This unexpected loss can be a humbling experience, reminding even the most skilled players that certainty is a fickle friend. Overconfidence can lead to a false sense of security, making the shock of losing even more profound—and, let's be honest, a bit of a gut punch.

I vividly recall playing in my parents' poker league one Wednesday evening many years ago. As an inexperienced player, my focus was solely on my own hand, a 9-high straight. I was practically patting myself on the back, thinking I was moments away from glorious victory. But here's the thing about poker: it's unpredictable, and just when you think you've got it all figured out, someone comes along with a better hand. In this case, that better hand was a full house—a combination of three of a kind and a pair, which is superior to a straight. The shock and disappointment I felt when I realized I wasn't the winner were profound. My confidence crumbled faster than a cookie in the hands of a toddler.

This experience mirrors a broader issue in parenting: *managing expectations*. Just as I was confident in my seemingly strong hand, parents often build up scenarios in their minds, envisioning perfect outcomes. We picture children laughing and playing nicely, the house running smoothly, and everyone on their best behavior. But as every parent knows, reality has a way of flipping the script. Things rarely go as planned, and when they don't, it can lead to feelings of disappointment and frustration.

Have you ever planned an activity for your children, only to watch it fall apart faster than a game of Jenga on a shaky table? You're filled with excitement, envisioning the joy and fun the activity will bring, not considering that your child might not share your enthusiasm. You've built up this perfect scenario in your head, expecting everything to go smoothly, and it can be incredibly disappointing when reality doesn't match those expectations.

I remember when we took our then 3-year-old son and infant daughter to an indoor water park. My husband and I were probably more excited than the children. We had planned it all out—splashing around, racing down slides, making memories that would last a lifetime. But as we walked through the entrance, we were greeted by the loud clang of bells and the thunderous splash of a giant bucket dumping water onto the park's equipment. What we thought would be a thrilling start to our adventure turned into a nightmare. The loud and unexpected splash terrified our son, sending him into a full-on tantrum that could have rivaled any soap opera drama.

Instead of enjoying the warm, fun-filled environment with the rest of the family, we spent our time in the cold, outdoor pool, far away from the dreaded bucket. For two days, we tried to coax him back inside, but nope—he was having none of it. Our idyllic family fun day had been replaced by a rather chilly experience that was, to put it mildly, not what we had envisioned. We left the water park feeling incredibly disappointed, not just because things hadn't gone according to plan, but because our expectations had set us up for that disappointment in the first place.

"In poker and parenting, sometimes the hand you're dealt isn't the one you were hoping for—but you've got to play it anyway."

This is where managing expectations becomes key. Just like in poker, where you can't always count on winning even with a good hand, in parenting, it's important to stay flexible and open-minded. Things aren't always going to go according to plan, and that's okay. The real trick is learning to roll with the punches, to adapt when things go sideways, and to find joy in the moments that don't go as expected.

---

"Sometimes the best memories are made when plans fall apart —and sometimes, the best poker hands are the ones you never saw coming."

---

This experience taught me a valuable lesson about managing expectations and understanding that sometimes, things don't go as envisioned. As parents, we often plan activities with the best intentions, hoping to create magical moments for our children. We imagine their delighted faces, the laughter, the memories that will last a lifetime. But here's the thing: children have their own personalities, fears, and preferences, which can sometimes lead to outcomes that are far from what we imagined. And that's okay.

Instead of feeling frustrated, it's important to adapt and find joy in the moments that do go well, even if they aren't the ones we originally planned. Flexibility and patience are key. It's about learning to pivot when things don't go as expected, and embracing the unexpected turns that life—and parenting—throw our way.

Just as in poker, where a bad beat is part of the game, in parenting, unexpected disappointments are part of the journey. These moments offer opportunities to learn, grow, and find new ways to connect with our children. Sometimes, the best experiences come from the most unplanned moments. It's about being present, rolling with the punches, and finding the silver lining in what might initially seem like a cloud.

REFLECTION QUESTIONS:

- Can you remember a time when you had high hopes for plans with your children, only for things to take an unexpected turn? How did the situation unfold?

- How did you and your family adjust when those plans didn't go as expected? What strategies helped you pivot and make the best of the moment?

- How did you and your children handle the disappointment? Were there any valuable lessons learned about flexibility, resilience, or finding joy in unexpected moments?

In poker, a bad beat offers an opportunity to learn and grow. You reassess your strategy, think about what went wrong, and prepare yourself for the next hand. In parenting, unexpected disappointments present similar chances to connect with children in new ways. Maybe that rained-out beach day turned into an epic indoor fort-building adventure. Or that failed movie night became an impromptu dance party in the living room.

This is why I emphasize the importance of managing expectations, being flexible, and finding joy in unplanned moments. These experiences teach parents and children valuable lessons in resilience and adaptability. After all, life isn't about sticking to a script; it's about improvising when the scene changes unexpectedly.

> "In parenting and poker, you can always find new ways to enjoy the game, whether you're winning or losing."

So the next time your perfectly planned day goes off the rails, remember that it's not about what you had planned—it's about how you respond when things don't go as expected. Take a deep breath, laugh it off, and look for the new opportunities that the unexpected has to offer. You might just find that those unplanned moments turn out to be the most memorable ones of all.

## CHECK AGAINST POWER

In poker, the term "check against power" refers to a strategic move where a player checks to see what the bet will be from a previous player who made a large or "powerful" bet in an earlier round. It's a move that acknowledges the influence and potential of the powerful player at the table, giving them space to reveal their next move before you make yours. It's all about understanding who holds the cards— literally and figuratively—and how that power can shape the game.

Similarly, in family dynamics, power and control can play significant roles in shaping behavior and relationships. Just as a player with significant power at the poker table can influence the game, the distribution of power within a family can greatly impact how everyone interacts with one another. When parents or children feel powerful— whether it's through making decisions, getting their way, or having a strong voice in the family—they often feel more secure and less anxious. Much like having a big stack of chips in poker: you've got more options, more room to maneuver, and a stronger sense of control over your environment.

But there's a flip side to all this power. If a child consistently gets what they want, they may feel powerful and secure, but they may also develop a sense of entitlement. In poker, an entitled player might make reckless bets, assuming their power will protect them. Similarly, an entitled child might struggle with empathy, finding it difficult to understand not getting their way. This lack of empathy can hinder their ability to connect with others and understand their feelings.

In poker, power dynamics are constantly shifting, requiring players to adapt their strategies on the fly. One minute you're the big stack, and the next, you're scrambling to stay in the game. In parenting, it's essential to manage power and expectations carefully to foster empathy and a balanced sense of self in children. Teaching children that they won't always get what they want isn't just about preparing them for disappointment—it's about helping them develop resilience and empathy. Experiencing moments of powerlessness can teach valuable lessons about understanding and compassion.

Consider the story of Emperor Kuzco from the movie The Emperor's New Groove. Kuzco, an all-powerful and arrogant emperor, planned to build a lavish summer home at the expense of demolishing a peasant's home. Pacha, the peasant, tried to explain the impact on his family, but Kuzco's power and entitlement blinded him to their plight. It wasn't until Kuzco was stripped of his power and forced to navigate the world from a new perspective that he began to understand and value others' feelings. Kuzco's journey to humility and empathy highlights the importance of understanding and valuing others' perspectives.

In real life, children must encounter situations where they don't always get what they want. These experiences help them appreciate what they have, understand others' perspectives, and develop empathy. It's like in poker—you can't win every hand, and sometimes you've got to fold, regroup, and learn from the experience. By managing power dynamics thoughtfully, parents can help children grow into compassionate, socially aware individuals capable of navigating life's complexities with understanding and empathy.

Just as a poker player must navigate power dynamics to succeed, parents must balance power and empathy to raise well-rounded, empathetic children. By teaching the value of considering others' feelings and the importance of coping with disappointment, we can guide children toward becoming compassionate and emotionally intelligent individuals.

---

"In poker and parenting, it's not just about holding the power—it's about knowing when to wield it and when to step back and listen."

---

REFLECTION QUESTIONS:

- Have you ever caught your kids acting like they're the rulers of their own little kingdoms, showing zero empathy for the hardworking peasants (aka you)? What was the situation, and how did you respond?

- Have you witnessed other children displaying entitlement—demanding the world on a silver platter without hesitation? How did that make you reflect on your own parenting approach?

- In what ways have you noticed entitlement or a lack of empathy in your own children? Are there specific triggers or situations where this behavior tends to surface?

- What strategies have you found helpful in teaching empathy and gratitude—before you start questioning whether you're raising a mini Emperor Kuzco?

Balancing power and empathy is a delicate dance, but it's one that can lead to incredible growth—for both parents and children. By "checking to the power" in your family dynamics, you can create an

## BALANCING SUPPORT AND RESPONSIBILITY

environment where everyone feels heard, valued, and capable of understanding and supporting each other.

## BALANCING SUPPORT AND RESPONSIBILITY

For several years of my professional life, I worked as an academic advisor and mental health counselor at a small liberal arts college. It was a job that often felt like playing a high-stakes game of poker, where I had to carefully balance my hand between supporting students in need and avoiding enabling their dependence—and, of course, dodging that pesky sense of entitlement that tends to creep in.

One incident that stands out involved a student who missed an exam because he was sick. Now, the course syllabus clearly stated that if you were going to miss an exam due to illness, you had to email the instructor beforehand. Simple enough, right? Well, this student missed that crucial step. When he found out that he wasn't allowed to make up the exam, he came to me angry and expected me to advocate on his behalf. He felt entitled to a makeup exam, despite not following the established protocol of notifying the instructor in advance. I could practically see the "But I'm special!" bubble floating above his head.

Now, here's where the balancing act came in. On one hand, I wanted to support the student and help him navigate his academic challenges. After all, I'm not a heartless robot. But on the other hand, I recognized the importance of adhering to policies and encouraging personal responsibility. The syllabus wasn't some ancient, dusty scroll that no one paid attention to—it was the playbook, and this student had fumbled the ball.

Advocating for him without considering the established guidelines would've been like letting a poker player sneak a few extra chips onto the table when no one was looking. Sure, it might make him happy in the moment, but it completely undermines the integrity of the game—and in this case, the integrity of the academic process.

So, I had to put on my best poker face and gently break it to him:

"I get that you're upset, but the rules are the rules. If we start bending them for one person, the whole game falls apart." Okay, I'm paraphrasing for an awesome effect, but you get the idea. The point was, he needed to learn that there are consequences for not following protocols, and those rules are there for a reason.

In my role, I had to balance empathy with enforcing boundaries. It was essential to communicate to the student that while I understood his frustration, the policy was clear and applied to all students equally. By doing so, I aimed to help him develop a sense of responsibility and an understanding of the importance of following rules.

Supporting the student by advocating for an exception would have been akin to allowing a poker player to disregard the rules, which undermines the integrity of the game. Instead, I chose to reinforce the importance of personal accountability and adherence to established policies. This approach helps students understand that their actions have consequences and that rules are in place to ensure fairness and consistency for everyone at the table.

---

"In poker and in life, bending the rules for one person would leave everyone at the table feeling cheated."

---

## BUILDING INDEPENDENCE

In poker, each player must rely on their own set of skills, make calculated decisions, and manage risks. No one's going to swoop in and play your hand for you. Similarly, as parents, we should encourage our children to develop their problem-solving abilities and learn to cope with anxiety on their own. Jumping in to solve every little problem for them or shielding them from even the slightest discomfort is like trying to play someone else's poker hand—it might feel helpful in the moment, but you're denying them the chance to learn and grow.

The essence of poker isn't about winning every hand; it's about developing the resilience and skill to navigate the ups and downs of the game. And let's be honest, no one's walking away from the table with a perfect record, but the lessons learned along the way? Priceless. This mirrors the process of building independence in children. The goal isn't to remove every obstacle from their path, but to teach them how to handle life's uncertainties with confidence. It's about giving them the tools they need to play their own hand, no matter what cards they're dealt.

I see this principle in action every day when my children are getting dressed. It can be so difficult not to help, and if I'm being totally honest, sometimes I do. I mean, who hasn't taken the shirt from their child and just put it over their head for them? Or held them up while you wrestle their pants on because, let's face it, we've got places to be and no one's got time for a half-hour sock struggle. But every time I step in, there's a little voice in the back of my head (and no, it's not just the one reminding me to add laundry detergent to the shopping list) saying, "You're not doing them any favors by stepping in."

By taking over these small tasks, I'm reinforcing the idea that they can't do these things themselves, that they need me to do it for them. And while it might seem trivial at the moment, it's part of a much bigger picture. We live in a generation where coping skills are often in short supply, and a big part of that is because we're so quick to step in and smooth out every wrinkle before our children even have a chance to try it on for size.

Now, I'm not saying we should overwhelm our children with anxiety or toss them into the deep end without a life jacket. But eliminating every trace of discomfort from their lives isn't doing them any favors either. Experiencing and managing discomfort is crucial for developing those all-important coping skills. It's like my role as an academic advisor, where I had to balance support with encouraging personal responsibility. As a parent, I need to allow my children to

# THE POKER PLAYER'S GUIDE TO PARENTING    41

face and manage their anxieties, even if it's as simple as putting on their own shoes.

Exposure to manageable levels of anxiety or discomfort can teach valuable lessons. It builds resilience and helps children learn that they're capable of overcoming difficulties—like finally mastering those tricky buttons on their shirts. This approach prepares them not just for academic success, but for life's broader challenges. It's a testament to the importance of allowing children to experience and learn from their struggles, ensuring they grow into independent, capable, and resilient adults.

By allowing children to experience manageable levels of discomfort and encouraging them to solve problems on their own, we're equipping them with the coping skills they'll need to handle bigger challenges later in life. So the next time you're tempted to swoop in and fix something for your children, remember that sometimes the best thing you can do is step back and let them figure it out on their own.

---

"It's not about playing the perfect game—it's about learning to play the hand you're dealt, all on your own."

---

REFLECTION QUESTIONS:

- Can you think of moments where you might have unintentionally encouraged dependence in your children? What were the circumstances, and how did you realize it?

- How do you create opportunities for your children to take the lead and build independence, even if it means letting go of perfection (like those mismatched socks)?

- What small changes could you make to help your children develop more confidence and self-reliance in their daily lives?

~

KEY LESSONS: MANAGING EXPECTATIONS

- **Bad Beats and Parenting Disappointments:** In poker, a "bad beat" is when you lose a hand you thought was in the bag. Similarly, in parenting, plans can go sideways faster than you can say, "Where did all the glitter come from?" Start today by embracing flexibility. When things don't go as planned, pivot like a pro and find alternative ways to enjoy time with your family— because sometimes the best moments are the unplanned ones.

- **Check Against Power:** In poker, "Check Against Power" means recognizing a strong player's influence at the table. In parenting, it's about managing power dynamics and fostering empathy. Teach your child today that they won't always get their way—because let's face it, life's not a 24/7 episode of *Children Rule the World*. Help them understand the value of empathy, resilience, and that sometimes, the word "no" is just as important as "yes."

- **Balancing Support and Responsibility:** Finding the sweet spot between being your child's biggest cheerleader and nudging them toward independence is key. Today, identify one way you can shift a little responsibility their way. Whether it's letting them tie

THE POKER PLAYER'S GUIDE TO PARENTING    43

their own shoes or remembering their homework without you hovering—give them the space to grow and learn that following rules and understanding consequences are all part of the game.

- **Building Independence:** Just like poker players rely on their own skills, parents should encourage children to tackle problems on their own—yes, even if it means a few more minutes of button-fumbling or sock-wrestling. Allow your child to struggle through a task today without swooping in like a superhero. They'll build resilience and problem-solving skills—and you'll get to drink your coffee while it's still hot. Win-win!

## PRACTICAL EXERCISE: MANAGING EXPECTATIONS

- **Reflect on a Recent Disappointment:** Think about a time when your plans with your children didn't go as expected. Write down what happened and how you adapted. What could you do differently next time to manage your expectations better?

- **Power Dynamics:** Identify a recent situation where your child was disappointed by not getting their way. Discuss with them how they felt and what they can learn about empathy and understanding others' perspectives.

- **Support vs. Responsibility:** Choose a task your child usually expects help with. Encourage them to complete it on their own this week. Afterwards, talk about how it made them feel and what they learned from the experience.

- **Building Independence:** Select an area where your child can be more self-reliant. Provide them with the tools and support they need, but let them handle the task. Reflect on the outcomes together and discuss any challenges they faced and overcame.

# CHAPTER 3

## BULLYING

In every type of relationship, there are individuals who exert dominance—whether at work, among peers, in significant relationships, or even in the world of poker. In poker, a bully is the player who likes to throw their weight around by raising the stakes, forcing out more cautious players or those with fewer chips. The chip leader—the player with the most chips at the table—is the king of the hill. With their massive stack, they can push other players around, making risky bets that others can't afford to match, all while casually sipping their drink and looking like they own the place.

As parents, we're the chip leaders of the household. We hold the power and have a significant influence over our children's decisions. Just like that chip leader in poker who can manipulate the game's outcome with a well-timed raise, parents can steer their children's choices with a well-placed consequence or reward. We might not be shoving all-in with a pair of Queens, but we've got our own tactics to keep things in line.

Take dinner time, for example. When my two oldest were 7 and 4, we were deep into the phase of discussing "good choices" and "bad choices." At these ages, they were starting to make their own decisions, but let's be real—I had the bigger chip stack. I could still manipulate their options to align with my preferences. I might say, "It's your choice whether or not you eat your dinner, but if you choose not to, you won't have any dessert." Boom—parental poker face. They get to feel like they're making the decision, but I'm still steering the ship, casually taking dessert off the table if they don't comply.

In poker, managing your chip stack means keeping a close eye on your resources compared to other players. It's all about power—more chips mean more power, and fewer chips mean less power. Chips give you options, just like power gives you options in life. But here's the twist: parental power might not always be as obvious as a giant pile of poker chips, but you can definitely sense it when your child holds the upper hand. You know that feeling—when it's just easier to do things for them rather than insisting they do it themselves, or when their relentless persistence grinds down your last nerve until you finally cave in. In those moments, it feels like they've got the bigger chip stack, and you're just trying to stay in the game. Your child became the bully, and you're the sad sap tearfully giving away your lunch money in hopes they don't play the card you fear most - in these circumstances, your children hold the upper hand. Maybe it's when they're refusing to go to bed, and you're too exhausted to argue, or when they're demanding that extra snack even though you know they're not hungry. It's those moments when you find yourself thinking, "How did I lose control of this game?"

REFLECTION QUESTIONS:

- Can you think of a time when you felt powerless as a parent—like your child had the bigger chip stack and was running the show? Was it during an epic bedtime battle or a meltdown that made you want to fold for the sake of peace?

- Have there been moments when you held the upper hand and played your chips just right—maybe by leveraging dessert privileges or cutting off screen time to reinforce a rule? What was the outcome?

- How do you navigate the constant power shifts in parenting, balancing authority with fairness while trying not to feel like you're negotiating with a tiny, emotionally charged poker pro?

- What strategies help you reclaim control without creating a battle of wills—and how do you decide when it's time to play hardball or let the small stuff slide?

"In poker and parenting, the chip stack might shift, but the game's all about how you play the hand you're dealt."

Remember, managing these dynamics is about more than just winning—it's about teaching your children how to navigate life's ups and downs, just like learning to play a good game of poker. Because whether you're playing for chips or dealing with bedtime negotiations, it's all about strategy, patience, and knowing when to hold 'em —or when to fold 'em.

## LOSING CONTROL OF THE TABLE

"Losing your stack" in poker is that dreaded moment when a player watches their chips dwindle away, ultimately losing their grip on the game. In the world of parenting, there's a similar experience—when you lose your authority and feel like you've lost control of the "parental table." It's that sinking feeling when you realize the dynamic has shifted, and suddenly your little one is calling the shots.

Children are quick learners, especially when it comes to figuring out what they can get away with. When respect isn't demanded, they learn not to give it. It's like letting your poker opponents see your hand every round—they're going to use that to their advantage, I mean - why wouldn't they? The same principle applies to relationships: if you don't expect respect, you won't receive it. And if you don't value yourself in your role as a parent, don't be surprised when your children start devaluing you too.

I remember an incident in a restaurant where a child was tearing into his mother for ordering the wrong menu item. Now, we've all been there—getting the wrong order is frustrating, especially when you've been eyeing those chicken nuggets all day. But the way this child was laying into his mom was like watching a Not a familiar reference. The poor mother, clearly mortified and eager to fix the mistake, seemed almost afraid of her son's anger. She was apologizing left and right, trying to appease him, while he continued to berate her like she was a phone rep requesting donations for firefighters, which believe me, I've personally done and experienced before.

Watching this play out, I couldn't help but wonder if this child had learned to use his anger as a weapon, knowing his mother would tolerate his disrespect just to keep the peace. It was like watching someone lose their entire stack in poker, one bad hand at a time—except here, it was a mother losing her authority, bit by bit, to a pint-sized power player.

Reflection Questions:

- Have you ever been publicly disrespected by your child—like during a full-blown grocery store protest, complete with foot-stomping and dramatic cries of injustice? How did you react in the moment?

- What thoughts ran through your mind as it happened? Was it a *"Thank goodness I'm not alone in this"* moment of solidarity with other parents, or more of an *"Oh no, not again"* situation?

- How did you choose to handle the situation—did you stand your ground, or did you fold just to make it through without causing a scene?

- Looking back, what did you learn from that experience about managing public outbursts while keeping your cool and reinforcing boundaries?

---

"In poker and parenting, losing your stack means losing control—time to reshuffle the deck and reclaim the table."

---

These moments are a reminder that, just like in poker, the key to maintaining control is setting boundaries and sticking to them. It's about making sure your children understand that respect isn't optional and that your authority is non-negotiable. Because in the end, the goal is to keep your stack—and your parental table—firmly in your control. These pint sized players are not your friends, so don't treat them as such.

## BALANCING ACTS: NAVIGATING PARENTAL CHALLENGES

When my oldest son was 7, every morning felt like a scene from an action movie—minus the explosions (though there were some days it came close). The challenge? Getting him, his younger sister, and baby brother to daycare before heading to work, which was a half-hour drive away. Picture this: the clock ticking down, the baby in one arm, my lunch and pump in the other, all while trying to corral two school-aged children who suddenly couldn't find their shoes—despite having worn them every single day of their lives. It was a minor miracle every time we made it out the door with everyone fully clothed and (mostly) prepared for the day.

One day, after what I thought was a particularly successful morning, I realized I had forgotten $1.00 for a fundraiser at my son's school. This dollar would allow him to wear a hat for the day. Desperately, I searched my purse for loose change but came up empty-handed. When I informed my son that I didn't have the money, he became very angry. Mom guilt set in, and I felt terrible that he couldn't participate in the fundraiser. I apologized profusely, but his anger grew, and he became hurtful in his words.

Finally, I'd had enough. "Have you ever made a mistake?" I asked, trying to keep my cool. He mumbled a reluctant "Yes," which was my cue to drop some parental wisdom. I wanted him to understand that while it's okay to feel angry, treating me like a punching bag was not. If I ignored his disrespect, I'd be setting a dangerous precedent. Luckily, my daycare provider swooped in like a hero with a spare dollar, saving the day and allowing my son to participate in the fundraiser. Crisis averted, but not without a few gray hairs gained.

Looking back, I wonder if I should have let my son cope with the disappointment, turning it into a lesson in empathy and resilience. But let's be honest, hindsight is 20/20, and in that moment, all I wanted was to resolve the situation before the tears (his and mine) started flowing.

It looks a bit different now that he's a pre-teen—the mistakes are less about midnight feedings and more about not getting the uniform clean in time or being late to pick him up from practice. But the underlying theme remains: if we allow ourselves to take all the blame, they'll certainly let us. Mistakes happen on both sides, and we need to remind ourselves of the power of reciprocated empathy.

> *What would you have done in this particular situation? Has your guilt ever prevented you from discussing with/ or disciplining your child?*

## THE VALUE OF BOUNDARIES AND RULES

Children may not consciously recognize it, and they certainly won't thank you for it in the heat of the moment, but deep down, I firmly believe they appreciate the presence of boundaries and rules. Somewhere in their core, they want to trust that someone is in control, even if they'd rather be in charge of the TV remote. Sure, the idea of a world without rules might seem like a blast at first—? No bedtimes? Unlimited snacks? All day YouTube? Everything goes—but even children understand that rules are necessary, whether they like to admit it or not.

Parents who try to be their child's best friend might enjoy a brief period of "cool parent" glory, but let's face it, that's not what children *need.* A best friend is someone who listens, loves, and supports—absolutely. But they're not responsible for teaching you to share your toys, use your inside voice, or understand that 3 AM is not an appropriate time for a Nintendo marathon. Children need consistency from someone who will love and support them while also correcting their behavior, even if it means occasionally transforming into the "mean" parent, every now and then.

This often means making decisions that will make the child angry, leading to eye rolls, stomping feet, and the classic, "You're ruining my life!" But those tough decisions are essential for teaching lessons and changing behaviors. As a therapist, it was tough to hear parents say they wanted to be their child's best friend because, newsflash, that's *not* in the job description. Children need someone who cares enough to set boundaries and rules for their protection and growth, not someone who's just along for the ride.

When my older children were 6 and 3, they loved riding their bikes like they were auditioning for the next Tour de France. But we lived in a neighborhood with a lot of construction, heavy equipment, and trucks that I feared would not notice young children zipping around on the road. So, I put my foot down: no riding on the road. Of course, they thought I was the "fun police," and their protestations were loud and dramatic. But after explaining my concerns—basically, that I didn't want them to get hit by a truck and die—we compromised. We'd either take their bikes to the park or I'd stand on the road like a traffic warden, ensuring no trucks were present while they rode. Once they understood my goal was their safety, the outrage dialed down a notch, and we found a solution that kept everyone (mostly) happy.

How do you react when you hear someone say, "My child is my best friend"? Does it make you cringe a little inside, or are you tempted to hand them a copy of *Parenting 101* with a few sections highlighted? And have you ever observed a parent/child relationship where the boundaries were as clear as mud? The kind where the child is running the show, and you're left wondering who's actually in charge?

At the liberal arts college where I worked for many years, we developed a highly involved advising model after identifying the increased needs of the collegiate student population. Advisors received alerts from all departments—academics, arts, athletics, and student affairs—about issues. They contacted students to address concerns or refer them to appropriate campus resources. Many students appreciated the involvement, but some were annoyed, saying, "I'm an adult and I'll make my own decisions." They had a point—how can you learn from your mistakes if someone else is always intervening?

Of course, the level of intervention needed for a child is worlds apart from that for a young adult. But if young adults are unprepared for collegiate life, would they really prefer advisors who ignored the warning signs? Would they rather we didn't care about their success or poor decision-making? The balance between guidance and independence is crucial as children grow into adults. It's the same balancing act parents face every day, knowing when to step in and when to let go.

As my oldest son transitioned into 6th grade, each student was provided with an iPad in order to have access to their academic learning system with syllabi and assignments as well as email. A far cry from the level of responsibility expected from elementary school. When he would be absent for a day or had a missing assignment, it was so difficult for us, as parents, not to take the lead on ensuring that he had it completed. It was now up to him to initiate those contacts and questions and ensuring for himself, that he was all caught up.

REFLECTION QUESTIONS:

- How do you recognize when it's time to let your child fail so they can learn an important lesson on their own? What signs help you make that decision?

- Can you recall a specific moment when you allowed your child to experience failure? How did it feel for you as a parent, and what was the outcome for your child?

- What lessons did both you and your child take away from that experience? How has it influenced your approach to supporting their growth and independence?

Remember, the goal isn't to be their best friend—it's to be their parent, the one who loves them enough to say no, set limits, and occasionally make the unpopular decisions that will help them grow into responsible, well-rounded adults. Because at the end of the day, that's the kind of "friend" they'll thank you for being.

## BOSSY PANTS

When my oldest son was 4, he hit me with a question I wasn't quite prepared for: "Mom, why do you always boss me around? You always tell me what to do." Now, I'll admit, I was a bit taken aback. It's not every day your preschooler confronts you with a mini existential crisis. But the child had a point—I couldn't exactly disagree with his observation.

So, I took a deep breath and leveled with him. "You know what, buddy? You're right. I *do* boss you around and tell you what to do." His eyes got a little wider, probably because he didn't expect me to agree so quickly. I went on to explain that when children are young and unable to make choices for themselves, parents intervene more frequently. As they grow older and start making their own (hopefully good) decisions, we gradually loosen the reins a bit. The goal is to trust them to navigate the world without needing constant intervention from us. But when you're 4 and your biggest concern is which dinosaur shirt to wear, someone's got to step in and help you figure it all out—and yes, that sometimes means being a bit bossy.

What he saw as bossy, I saw as part of the learning and nurturing process. I wanted him to understand that, sure, part of my job as his mom is to give directions and set boundaries, but there's a lot more to it. I told him that being a mom also means playing with police cars (even when I'm secretly wishing for a nap), reading books together, snuggling up while watching TV, and tucking him in at night. It's all part of the package deal.

---

*"In the game of parenting, being 'bossy' just means you're the referee, the coach, and the cheerleader—all rolled into one."*

---

## CHIPPING AWAY AT THE CHIP LEADER

In poker, "chipping away" at the chip leader means that a player with fewer chips is slowly but surely gaining ground, bit by bit, until they start to close the gap. It's a game of patience and strategy—much like parenting when you're at an authority or power deficit. Sometimes, as parents, we feel like we're losing ground, like the children have the bigger stack and we're just trying to stay in the game. But with steady, incremental changes, you can start chipping away at that deficit, gradually setting boundaries and demanding more respect. It's all about making slow and steady progress, just like that persistent poker player who keeps edging closer to the chip leader's throne.

Potty training is the ultimate test of patience and incremental progress. It's a prime example of chipping away at a huge deficit. For years, your little one has been blissfully using diapers without a care in the world, no consequences, no pressure. Then, one day, you roll out the potty and introduce this strange new contraption, and it's like, "Wait, you want me to do what now?"

Just as a chip leader fights to stay ahead, a child might resist giving up diapers because, let's face it, they're comfortable with what they know. The cozy, no-strings-attached life of diapers is hard to give up. So, you start small. The first victory? Just getting them to sit on the potty—cue the wild applause and exaggerated "Yay!" Positive reinforcement becomes your best friend, turning every tiny success into a reason to celebrate. Over time, that slow and steady progress starts to add up, and before you know it, you're down to just one emergency diaper in the car (for old times' sake).

It's all about reinforcing incremental progress. Maybe they didn't go, but hey, they sat on the potty without making a run for it. That's a win! Over time, those small victories start to stack up, and suddenly, that daunting mountain of potty training doesn't seem so insurmountable anymore. It's the same with any parenting challenge—acknowledging progress, no matter how small, helps your child feel validated and motivated to keep going. They might not be where you want them to be yet, but with consistent reinforcement of those small achievements, they'll get there.

So, can you think of an example with your own children where there was an issue you seemingly "chipped away" at? Maybe it was something that felt daunting at first—like getting them to sleep in their own bed or tackling a tough homework routine—but with slow and steady progress, things started to get better. What was it like for you? How did you reinforce those small victories along the way?

> "In poker and parenting, it's not about winning every hand—it's about making the most of the chips you've got and knowing that slow and steady can still win the game."

Remember, every small step forward is *progress*. Whether it's potty training, setting boundaries, or helping your teen navigate their way through a tough school year, chipping away at the challenge is how you eventually turn the tide. So keep clapping, keep reinforcing, and keep moving forward—because those little victories are what lead to the big wins in the end.

## CASHING OUT: KNOWING WHEN TO QUIT WHILE YOU'RE AHEAD

In poker, "cashing out" is the glorious moment when a player decides to leave the table and exchange their accumulated chips for cold, hard cash. Sometimes, they walk away with more money than they started with, beaming with the satisfaction of having played their cards right. Other times, they cash out with less, trying to minimize their losses before things take a nosedive. It's all about knowing when to make your exit and, as they say, "quit while you're ahead."

In the wild world of parenting, the "quit while you're ahead" mentality can be a lifesaver when managing your children's behavior. You know that moment when you ask something of your child, they actually comply without a fuss, and you think, "Hey, I'm on a roll here!" But then, just as you're about to push your luck by asking for one more thing, you remember: this could go south real quick. That's when you take your metaphorical chips and cash out, happy to leave on a high note.

I not only lost my cool, but I lost an opportunity to teach her how to behave better. With three young children, it was always a game of high-stakes parenting to gauge how long good behavior—or more specifically, a good mood—would last. This was especially true when my youngest son was nearing his first birthday. We knew that his good mood was a ticking time bomb, and once that fuse ran out, well, let's just say things could get explosive. So, we'd time our outings, events, or any time out of the house with military precision, aiming to leave before that adorable grin turned into a full-blown meltdown.

Most parents can relate to this strategy. You've made it through a day at the zoo, the children have seen the lions, giraffes and red pandas, eaten their snacks without any major messes, and no one has had a major meltdown yet. You're feeling good—like maybe, just maybe, you've got this whole parenting thing figured out. But then you catch a glimpse of the clock and realize you're entering the danger zone: nap time is looming, energy levels are dropping, and you're one minor incident away from an epic tantrum in front of the monkey exhibit. That's when you make the call to cash out, pack up, and head home before the magic wears off.

**Can you think of an example where you managed to quit while you were ahead?** Maybe you wrapped up a playdate just before things got messy, or you left a family gathering right before your toddler decided to test the acoustics with a high-pitched scream. And what about those times when you didn't quit while you were ahead and found yourself knee-deep in trouble? What are the warning signs in your children that help you decide when it's time to make a graceful exit?

> "Do the Seinfeld thing, leave on a high note"

As parents, we learn to read the signs. Maybe it's that slightly glazed-over look in their eyes, the way they start to drag their feet, or the infamous "I'm not tired" declaration that we all know is code for "I'm about to lose it." Recognizing those signals and deciding to call it a day can save you from turning a great day into a not-so-great one.

## KEY LESSONS: THE BENEFITS OF BULLYING

- **Dominance:** Recognize when and how to use your authority effectively. Think of it as your parental poker face—guide your child's choices by presenting options that secretly align with what you want. Today, try framing a choice for your child in a way that nudges them toward your desired outcome. It's a win-win!

- **Losing Control:** Maintain your parental authority, even when it feels like the children are stacking up chips and you're just hanging on. Reflect on a recent situation where you felt powerless, and then channel your inner poker pro to develop a strategy for regaining control. This might involve setting clear expectations and, more importantly, following through with consistent consequences. Remember, you're the dealer—keep those cards close to your chest!

- **Balancing Acts:** Balancing empathy with discipline is the ultimate parenting tightrope walk. When you feel that all-too-familiar "mom guilt" creeping in, remind yourself that setting boundaries and enforcing rules isn't just about being the bad cop—it's about ensuring your child's long-term well-being. So the next time you're tempted to cave in, remember: rules today, responsible adults tomorrow.

- **The Value of Boundaries and Rules:** Establish and maintain clear boundaries. Communicate with your child why rules are important—because, let's face it, they might not see the wisdom in "no dessert before dinner" right away. Explain that your job is to protect and guide them. After all, every game needs rules to keep it from descending into chaos, and the same goes for family life.

- **Chipping Away at the Chip Leader:** Implement incremental changes to regain authority, much like chipping away at a chip leader's stack in poker. Identify one behavior you want to improve in your child—maybe it's getting them to clean up their toys without being asked 47 times—and start making small, consistent efforts to address it. Over time, you'll see progress, and before you know it, they'll be tidying up like a pro (or at least with minimal grumbling).

- **Cashing Out:** Know when to stop pushing. Recognize your child's limits and choose to "quit while you're ahead" by ending great rolls on a positive note before things go south. It's all about knowing when to cash out with everyone still smiling.

## PRACTICAL EXERCISE: MANAGING POWER DYNAMICS

- **Reflect on Dominance and Influence:** Identify a recent situation where you successfully guided your child's behavior using your authority. How did you frame the options, and what was the outcome?

- **Regain Control:** Think of a time you felt powerless as a parent. Develop a plan to regain control by setting clear, non-negotiable rules and consistent consequences.

- **Balance Empathy with Discipline:** Recall a situation where "mom guilt" influenced your decision. How can you balance empathy with the need for discipline in similar future situations?

- **Communicate Boundaries:** Choose a current rule or boundary and explain to your child why it is important. Reinforce the message that your role includes protecting and guiding them.

- **Incremental Changes:** Identify a behavior you want to improve in your child. Start making small, consistent efforts to address it, and track the progress over time.

- **Quit While You're Ahead:** Reflect on a recent family outing or activity. Did you recognize and act on your child's limits? How can you better gauge when to end activities on a high note in the future?

By understanding and implementing these key lessons, parents can better manage power dynamics, set effective boundaries, and foster resilience and independence in their children.

# CHAPTER 4

## MY MY MY POKER FACE

P hil Ivey, a renowned poker player, is famous for his impeccable poker face—a blank expression that reveals nothing about his hand. In the high-stakes world of poker, if a player even hints at excitement when dealt a great hand—whether it's a subtle widening of the eyes or a tiny smirk—it can tip off other players, causing them to fold faster than you can say, "Royal flush!"

Players who have perfected their poker face make it nearly impossible for opponents to read their hand. And just like these poker pros, parents, too, must master the art of the poker face. But unlike poker players, our goal isn't to hide our hand from our children —it's to avoid showing vulnerability or conveying the wrong impression. Because let's be real, children are like tiny mind-readers who can sniff out weakness a mile away.

I remember a time when I was disciplining my son—though, to be honest, the specifics of what he did have long since faded into the chaotic blur that is parenthood. My go-to method was a time-out, typically lasting 1-5 minutes. And let me tell you, those 5 minutes felt like an eternity, not just for him but for me, too. There he was, sitting on the time-out spot, crying with the saddest face I had ever seen, his big, teary eyes looking up at me like I had just canceled Christmas.

Every fiber of my being wanted to give in. I wanted to scoop him up, hug him, and let him go back to playing as if nothing had happened. But I didn't. I knew that if I gave in, I'd be setting a dangerous precedent—one that said, "Hey, throw a little tantrum, and all your troubles will go away!" So I summoned every ounce of willpower and maintained the best poker face I could manage. No smile, no expression, no vulnerability. I was like a statue—a very conflicted, emotionally tormented statue.

Inside, I was battling an emotional storm. My heart was breaking, worried he might hate me or think I didn't love him. But I couldn't let it show. Just like a poker player doesn't want to reveal their hand, I didn't want to reveal my thoughts. Because here's the thing: if my son knew how I really felt—if he caught even a hint of my inner turmoil—he would have realized he could manipulate me with that sad puppy face. And trust me, children are quick to pick up on these things. They're smart and perceptive; if they see even the slightest crack in your poker face—a smile, a sigh, a softening of the eyes—they know they've won. They know you won't follow through, and in that moment, they hold all the power. They've won the hand, and you're left scrambling to regain control of the table.

So, when has your inability to maintain a good poker face ruined any hope for disciplinary action? Maybe it was that time you tried to stay serious while your child, mid-tantrum, said something unintentionally hilarious, and you couldn't help but crack a smile. Or perhaps it was when their crocodile tears got the best of you, and you caved in, letting them have their way just to stop the waterworks. Whatever the situation, we've all been there—trying to keep a straight face while our emotions are doing the cha-cha inside.

---

"In poker and parenting, the game isn't over until you master the poker face—because those little sharks are watching your every move."

---

The truth is, maintaining that poker face is tough, but it's crucial for setting boundaries and teaching lessons. Children need to know that you mean business when it comes to discipline, and that starts with not giving away your hand—no matter how much they turn on the charm. So, the next time you're faced with a test of your parental poker face, take a deep breath, channel your inner Phil Ivey, and remember that a straight face today can mean smoother sailing tomorrow.

## THE IMPORTANCE OF MANAGING EMOTIONAL REACTIVITY

Having a good poker face isn't just about looking cool while holding a pair of deuces —it's about managing your emotional reactivity, keeping your internal dialogue from spilling out onto the table for everyone to see. Similarly, in parenting, keeping a lid on those emotions is crucial if you want to steer the ship without hitting an iceberg.

If you can't manage your emotional reactivity, you might end up frightening your children more than teaching them. Just like in poker, where losing your cool loses you respect, as a parent, losing your temper can lead to losing your child's respect. And, let's be honest, you might even end up modeling the very behavior you're trying to eliminate. It's like telling them not to eat cookies before dinner with crumbs still on your lips.

My daughter participated in 3rd-4th grade volleyball and at that time, I was helping coach her team. Something I would usually really enjoy, but, at this particular game, my daughter wasn't playing well and her attitude was matching. Anytime that I would give her some feedback, she made these annoyed faces and was disrespecting both me and her teammates. I thought I might lose it in front of an entire gym of unsuspecting spectators. My internal emotional reactivity rivaled the character "anger" from the Inside Out movie. All I could think was, "I did not raise her to act like this."

Many parents would agree: while children have a remarkable talent for forgetting where they put their socks and shoes, they have a near-photographic memory for those moments when we lost our cool. Those high-octane moments? They're etched into their little minds like a bad tattoo.

I remember a time when my oldest son was six. He got frustrated over something my daughter did—probably something earth-shattering like her breathing too close to his Lego masterpiece. He bent down to her height, squared his little shoulders, and unleashed his rage right in her face. I could feel the frustration bubbling up inside me, and before I knew it, I was bending down to his height and yelling, "Get out of your sister's face and stop yelling at her!" Oh, the irony. I had just scolded him for the exact behavior I was modeling. The teachable moment slipped through my fingers, and instead of diffusing the situation, I ended up scaring both of them—mission not accomplished.

---

"it's not just about holding your cards—it's about holding your temper, too."

---

The truth is, we're all human, and sometimes our emotions get the better of us. But it's important to remember that those moments are teaching opportunities, not just for our children but for us as well. The next time you feel that frustration rising, take a deep breath, channel your inner poker pro, and remember that managing your emotional reactivity is key to winning the long game. Because in the end, parenting is less about playing the perfect hand and more about how you handle the cards you're dealt.

REFLECTION QUESTIONS:

- Can you remember a time when your emotional reaction frightened your children? What triggered that response, and how did the situation unfold?

- How did you feel afterward—guilty, reflective, or perhaps motivated to approach things differently next time?

- What steps did you take to address the situation with your children? How did you use that experience to grow as a parent and strengthen your connection with them?

## USING A POKER FACE TO MASK THEM LOL'S

The poker face isn't just a tool for hiding emotional reactivity; it's also a lifeline for masking laughter—especially when your child says or does something wildly inappropriate but undeniably hilarious. We've all been there: your child drops a word or pulls a stunt, and suddenly you're caught between the urge to burst out laughing and the need to correct the behavior.

Take, for example, the first time you hear your child say a curse word. It's shockingly funny to hear a tiny human drop an f-bomb with the same casual ease as they might say, "Pass the ketchup." But here's the catch—if you laugh, you're basically signing up for a future filled with your little one experimenting with colorful language at the most inopportune moments. And let's be honest, there's nothing like a well-timed curse word to spice up a Thanksgiving dinner with the family.

One evening, when my oldest son was six, he was sitting at the counter eating supper, and out of nowhere, he said, "Ah, f***, I'm tired." My husband and I immediately exchanged those parental wide-eyed looks, the ones that say, "Did he really just say that?" while simultaneously biting our tongues to hold back the laughter threatening to burst out. I mean, the child was clearly channeling his inner grumpy old man, and it was pure comedy gold. He literally could have been the exact replica of his grandpa, sitting in his chair, cursing at the TV.

But I knew this was a crucial moment. I had to keep a straight face, even though my insides were doing cartwheels. So, I asked him calmly, "Do you know what you just said?" Of course, he repeated it, still completely unaware that his language had just crossed into Rated-R territory. That's when I explained that the word "f***" was a naughty word and that he would be in trouble if he used it again. He looked at me, utterly bewildered by the fuss, and immediately blamed the big children on the bus for his newfound vocabulary.

The whole time, I was mentally high-fiving myself for not cracking a smile because if he'd seen me laughing, it would've been game over. He'd be dropping f-bombs left and right, figuring it was just another way to get a chuckle out of Mom and Dad. But by keeping my poker face firmly in place, I managed to nip that little experiment in the bud—no matter how hard it was not to laugh.

REFLECTION QUESTIONS:

- Can you recall a time when your child did something clearly wrong but so hilariously unexpected that it was hard to keep a straight face? What happened in that moment?

- Were you able to maintain your poker face, or did the laughter slip through despite your best efforts? How did your child react?

- How do you balance addressing misbehavior while also

appreciating those genuinely funny parenting moments that make the journey memorable?

## USING A POKER FACE TO MASK EMOTIONS

Poker faces aren't just for stifling giggles when your child says something hilariously inappropriate; they're also handy when you feel like you might cry. Now, I'll be the first to say that I have mixed feelings about this. After all, I don't want to discourage crying—tears are a natural, healthy way to process emotions. But there are definitely times when putting on that poker face is necessary, especially when you're dealing with anxiety or grief that you don't want your children to experience.

In situations where a parent is grieving or has experienced a loss, it's a delicate balancing act to manage the display of emotions. As a therapist I know how important it is to show children that emotional pain is real, that it's okay to cry, and that expressing grief is part of the healing process. But at the same time, intense grief, especially when it involves a lot of tears, can be unnerving for children. They might start to worry about you, and their anxiety can ramp up faster than a toddler's sugar high after a birthday party.

So, what's the solution? It's crucial to model emotional resilience for your children. This doesn't mean pretending everything's fine when it's not, but rather showing them that, while it's okay to cry and feel sad, there's also strength in maintaining composure. It's about finding that balance—crying when you need to, but also reassuring your children that, despite the sadness, everything will eventually be okay. This helps them understand and process their own emotions without feeling like they need to take care of you.

## REFLECTION QUESTIONS:

- Can you recall a time when you cried in front of your children? What led to that moment, and how did it unfold?

- How did your children react—did they offer comfort, show concern, or seem unsure of how to respond?

- What was that experience like for you as a parent? Did you feel a sense of relief in showing your vulnerability, or did it bring feelings of guilt or hesitation?

- How has that moment influenced the way you approach emotional openness and vulnerability with your children moving forward?

And then there's the flip side—have you ever felt the need to hide your emotions from your children, to put on that poker face even when you were feeling like a mess inside? Maybe it was because you didn't want to burden them with your grief, or perhaps you were trying to keep things light and normal during a tough time. Whatever the reason, what was your reasoning behind it, and how did it make you feel afterward?

"Sometimes the hardest bluff to pull off is the one where you're trying to hide your own heartache."

The reality is, we're all just doing our best to navigate this emotional rollercoaster called life, and that includes figuring out when to let our children see us cry and when to put on a brave face.

The key is to remember that it's okay to show them that emotions are real and that it's okay to feel sad, but it's also important to show them that even in the darkest times, there's hope and strength to be found.

## USING A POKER FACE TO MANAGE DISCIPLINARY REACTIONS

A parental poker face is a secret weapon in the art of managing your immediate reactions to your child's behavior. While quick reflexes are a must when your child is reaching for a hot stove, they're less crucial during disciplinary moments. In fact, being too reactive can sometimes overshadow the lesson you're trying to teach. It's hard for a child to grasp why they're in the wrong when they're more focused on your emotional outburst than the actual issue at hand.

Let me paint a picture for you. When my oldest son was seven, we came home one Sunday evening after a long weekend at my parents' house. My husband and I were dragging—we'd just spent the last two hours wrangling children, luggage, and a trunk full of snacks from Grandma's pantry. As any parent knows, unpacking after a trip is its own special kind of torture, especially when all you really want to do is collapse on the couch.

My son had taken a bath and was now dozing off on the couch, mid-movie, eyes half-closed, and clearly overtired. I did what any sensible parent would do—I picked him up and carried him to bed. But instead of being grateful for a little extra shut-eye, he was mad. *Really* mad. As I tucked him in and tried to give him a goodnight kiss, he shot me an angry glare that could've rivaled a teenage drama queen.

Now, my first instinct was to mirror that glare right back at him. My internal dialogue was on fire: "How dare he be rude to me after we just spent the entire weekend making sure he had a blast? We're exhausted, we've got a week of work ahead, and this is the thanks I get? God forbid I put him to bed when he's clearly about to conk out on the couch!"

I wanted to snap back, to let my frustration show, but I knew better. If I gave in to that impulse, he wouldn't hear a word of what I was saying. He'd just see my anger and double down on his own. So instead, I put on my best poker face, took a deep breath, and calmly told him that his angry glares were hurtful. Then I kissed him on the forehead (despite his best attempts to squirm away) and walked out of the room.

It wasn't long before he came out to apologize, his earlier frustration melted away. By not reacting emotionally, I gave him the space to reflect on his actions. He was able to understand that what he did was wrong, and more importantly, he felt comfortable enough to make amends. *The less reactive you are when disciplining, the more receptive your child is likely to be.* It's a bit like playing a strategic hand of poker—calm, deliberate actions can lead to a winning outcome.

In those moments, conscious, deliberate discipline allows parents to communicate their concerns in a way that's more likely to be heard and understood. And honestly, it's way more effective than a full-blown showdown.

So the next time your child gives you that "how dare you" look, take a deep breath, channel your inner poker player, and remember that staying calm will not only help you get through the moment, but it'll also teach your child a valuable lesson in emotional regulation.

---

"It's not the loudest player who wins—it's the one who keeps their cool."

---

## THE ART OF BLUFFING IN PARENTING

In poker, a bluff is when a player bets big on a hand that's, well, pretty mediocre. The goal? To make everyone else at the table think they're holding the nuts (poker lingo for the best possible hand). It's all about deception—getting the other players to fold and hand you the pot without having to show your cards. But here's the thing:

bluffing isn't just for poker tables. In fact, bluffing is something parents do all the time, and usually, it's not to win a game but to keep the family train on the tracks.

Take the tale of Santa Claus, for example. Parents across the globe have been pulling off the ultimate bluff for generations, convincing their children that a jolly guy in a red suit is watching their every move and deciding whether they deserve presents or a lump of coal on Christmas morning. And let's face it, the mere mention of Santa's "naughty or nice" list can whip any child's behavior into shape.

But the difference between a poker bluff and a parental bluff is all in the intention. In poker, you're bluffing to win the game, while in parenting, you might be bluffing to foster a little magic or, more realistically, to modify behavior when your patience is wearing thin.

Parental bluffs can also serve a protective purpose. Sometimes they take the form of emotional disguise, where you shield your children from your own feelings to keep them safe and secure. For instance, one winter, I was driving my 4-year-old son and 2-year-old daughter to daycare on icy roads that could've doubled as an ice-skating rink. I'm an anxious winter driver at the best of times, but this particular day had my knuckles turning white on the steering wheel. As we approached a highway intersection, the car started to slide, and my heart was pounding out of my chest. But instead of letting them see my fear, I pulled off the ultimate bluff. I plastered on a smile and turned the whole thing into a fun ride, making them laugh and enjoy the experience. They thought we were on some kind of snowy adventure, while I was silently praying we'd make it to daycare in one piece. Bluff: successful. Fear: hidden.

Then there was the time my 4-year-old son came home from daycare, urgently requesting a haircut because a boy had made fun of his curly hair. My initial reaction was a cocktail of disappointment, sadness, and a sprinkle of mama-bear anger toward the child who'd made my son feel bad. But instead of letting him see my true feelings, I put on my poker face. I calmly explained that we shouldn't let other people's opinions dictate how we feel about ourselves, all the while maintaining a steady, comforting tone. Afterward, when he was out of sight, I went to my closet and cried—heartbroken that he had to experience that kind of pain at such a young age. Bluff: executed flawlessly. Emotions: bottled up for later.

REFLECTION QUESTIONS:

- Have you ever "bluffed" your kids—like claiming the TV was broken because your brain couldn't survive another episode of *Paw Patrol*? What drove you to pull that little parental sleight of hand?

- Did your kids fall for it, or did they see through your poker face like tiny, suspicious detectives?

- Was your bluff a win, or did it backfire spectacularly? Looking back, would you play the same hand again?

- How do you juggle these harmless fibs while teaching your kids the importance of honesty—without accidentally raising future card sharks?

---

"Sometimes the biggest bluffs are the ones we pull to protect the ones we love."

---

The art of bluffing in parenting isn't about deception for the sake of it —it's about guiding, protecting, and sometimes just getting through the day with your sanity intact. Whether it's hiding your fear on an icy road or pretending the crusty old elf on the shelf is real, these little bluffs are part of what keeps the family game running smoothly.

## THE DYNAMICS OF BAITING IN PARENTING

In poker, "baiting" is when you throw out a bet designed to lure your opponent into a trap, giving them just enough rope to hang themselves. It's like dangling a juicy worm in front of a fish, knowing full well they're going to take the bait and end up as dinner. Poker players bait each other to entice their opponents into betting, all the while knowing they've got the winning hand. But here's the kicker—baiting isn't just for poker tables or fishing trips; it happens all the time in parenting.

Baiting in parenting involves a delicate mix of patience and strategy, with the inevitable goal of wearing down your opponent—who, in this case, is *you*. If you've ever been locked in a prolonged argument with your child, you know exactly what I'm talking about. It's like you're the fish at the end of the line, thrashing around with all your might until, exhausted, you finally give in and let yourself be reeled in. The longer the argument drags on, the more power your child gains, because each minute that ticks by is more time they have to convince you to change your decision or cave to their demands. And eventually, you reach that moment where you think, "Is this really worth it?" and—boom—just like that, they've won. Collective sigh.

I remember a time when my son decided to pull off the ultimate baiting strategy. He had just received a brand-new holiday train set, one of those elaborate ones that looked like it needed a degree in engineering to assemble. My husband and I, after a long day of holiday festivities, were finally settling in to watch a TV show, craving just one hour of uninterrupted peace. But our son had other plans. He came in, all wide-eyed and hopeful, asking if we could help him put the train together. We politely declined, asking him to play with something else for a while.

But like a seasoned poker player who knows how to read the table, he didn't give up. A few minutes later, he was back, asking again. And then again. And again. Each time, our frustration grew,

74    LEAHA HAMMER

and our focus on the TV show waned. Finally, after what felt like the tenth interruption, my husband, in a fit of exasperation, shut off the TV, stormed into our son's room, and started assembling the train.

Our son, of course, was thrilled. He had successfully baited us into doing exactly what he wanted. He knew that by prolonging the fight and wearing us down, he would eventually get his way. Instead of shutting down his request early on, we let ourselves get caught in his web of persistence. He set the lure, waited patiently, and caught us in a moment of frustration and vulnerability. We stayed on the line, and he reeled us in, hook, line, and sinker.

So, what's the takeaway here? Children know exactly how to push our buttons to get what they want. The longer you stay in the argument, the more likely you are to cave. The key is to recognize when you're being baited and shut it down before you find yourself putting together a train set when all you really wanted was to enjoy a quiet evening.

KEY LESSONS

- **The Poker Face in Parenting:** Just like poker pros use a blank expression to hide their hand, parents must master their own poker face to avoid showing vulnerability to their children. Practice maintaining a neutral expression when disciplining your child, even when their antics are pushing all your buttons.

- **Managing Emotional Reactivity:** Keeping a lid on your emotions is key to maintaining authority and teaching valuable lessons. If you lose your cool, you might end up modeling the very behavior you're trying to correct. Reflect on a recent time when your emotions got the better of you—what could you have done differently to stay calm? Next time, try channeling your inner poker player to keep your reactions in check.

- **Bluffing in Parenting:** Bluffing isn't just for poker—it's a tool parents use daily to guide behavior and maintain peace. Whether it's spinning a tale about Santa's "naughty or nice" list or masking your own fear to keep your child calm, these little bluffs help keep the family running smoothly. Think about a time you successfully "bluffed" your child—how did it help in that moment?

- **Masking Laughter:** Sometimes, your child's behavior is so unexpectedly funny that it takes everything in you not to laugh. But letting that laughter slip can undermine your authority. The next time your child says something hilariously inappropriate, remember to hold that poker face. Practice stifling your giggles and addressing the behavior calmly, so they don't get mixed signals.

- **Using a Poker Face to Manage Discipline:** Being too reactive during disciplinary moments can overshadow the lesson you're trying to teach. When your child gives you that "how dare you" look, resist the urge to react emotionally. Instead, maintain a calm, neutral demeanor, and focus on communicating the lesson clearly. Remember, staying cool under pressure can lead to better outcomes in the long run.

# CHAPTER 5

## SOCIAL AWARENESS

In poker, seasoned players know that success isn't just about the cards in their hand. It's also about reading their opponents—deciphering their actions, emotions, and potential strategies. This broader awareness allows them to make strategic decisions, factoring in the possible moves of others at the table. Parenting, much like poker, benefits from a similar kind of awareness, but it's not just about being aware of one's self—it's about *social* awareness, the ability to understand and empathize with the feelings, thoughts, and experiences of others.

In poker, players look for tells—subtle physical or verbal cues that might give away information about another player's hand. A slight change in breathing, a shift in posture, or even how someone handles their chips can provide valuable insights. Poker greats like Phil Hellmuth emphasize the importance of *consistency* in behavior; if an opponent always acts a certain way when they're bluffing or holding a strong hand, that pattern becomes a valuable tell. Similarly, betting patterns reveal a lot about a player's strategy. Daniel Negreanu, known for his exceptional ability to read betting patterns, often suggests paying attention to not just the size of the bets but also the timing and rhythm. A quick, confident bet might indicate strength, while hesitation could suggest a bluff.

Understanding the overall dynamics at the table—knowing who's comfortable, who's on tilt, and who's out of their element—can give good poker players an edge in reading the game.

Translating these poker skills into parenting, we find that social awareness is about much more than just recognizing when a child is upset. It involves understanding the broader social context in which these emotions arise and helping children navigate these complexities. It's about fostering empathy, perspective-taking, and communication skills. For example, when a child sees a friend who is upset, a socially aware response might be to ask if they're okay, rather than trying to cheer them up. Encouraging children to think about how their actions affect others can help them develop a deeper sense of empathy and responsibility.

Building this awareness in children isn't always easy. As a therapist, I've often found that teaching social awareness is one of the more challenging aspects of my work. It requires us to step outside of our comfort zones and consider perspectives that might not validate our own. Children, being naturally egocentric, often see the world through the lens of their own needs and desires. And who can blame them? When you're 4 years old, the biggest crisis in life might be a broken crayon or, heaven forbid, *Netflix* not streaming fast enough— empathy takes time to develop.

I remember vividly when my two older children were seven and four, and my youngest was just a baby. Simple outings like trips to the park, the pool, or a parade became logistical challenges. The baby couldn't participate in the same way, and my older children couldn't quite grasp why these outings had suddenly become more complicated. To them, it was just, "Why can't we go to the pool right now?" while I was juggling a million new responsibilities as a nursing mother. Their world hadn't changed, but mine had—dramatically. They couldn't yet see beyond their own experiences to understand how the presence of a baby had shifted the dynamics for everyone.

Even now, as they are older, my older two want to go on a bike ride, but their 6-year-old younger brother can't keep up. They still struggle with empathy and empathic perspectives, because it doesn't match their personal agendas.

But then there are those moments when all the teaching, the patience, and the endless explanations pay off. I recall a time when my oldest, then 7, asked if he could have one of the Gatorades in the fridge. My husband had bought them for himself, needing them to stay hydrated while working in a factory with extreme heat. When my husband explained this to our son, his response was unexpected and heartwarming: "Okay, I understand. You need it more than I do." Cue the parental victory dance. In that moment, my son demonstrated a level of social awareness that felt like hitting the jackpot in parenting. He was able to see beyond his own immediate desire and recognize someone else's need as more pressing. It was a small moment, but it felt monumental—proof that all those conversations about thinking of others were actually sinking in. More recently, my daughter was at an amusement park and won two stuffies and when she saw how disappointed my youngest son was, she gave one of her stuffies to him. (The less preferable one, but a win, regardless.)

REFLECTION QUESTIONS:

- Have you caught moments where your child showed real social awareness—like comforting a friend who was feeling down—or completely missed the mark, like throwing a full-blown meltdown over the last slice of pizza?

- What challenges have you faced while trying to help them develop those essential social skills? Are there certain situations that seem to trip them up every time?

THE POKER PLAYER'S GUIDE TO PARENTING 79

- What small victories have made you think, *"Hey, maybe I'm actually nailing this parenting thing"*? How do those moments encourage you to keep guiding them along the way?

- How do you balance letting them learn through social slip-ups while still offering the support they need to grow?

In both poker and parenting, mastering social awareness is a game-changer. For poker players, it's about reading the room and making strategic decisions based on others' behavior. For parents, it's about helping children develop empathy, understand different perspectives, and communicate effectively. By teaching your children the skills of social awareness, you're not just preparing them for social interactions—you're equipping them with the tools to navigate life's challenges with empathy, understanding, and strategic thinking. Whether it's at the poker table or in the everyday interactions of life, understanding what's in your hand and what might be in someone else's is key to success.

## PRACTICAL EXERCISES FOR DEVELOPING SOCIAL AWARENESS

- **Observational Practice:** Just as poker players observe others at the table, encourage your child to observe people around them. Ask them to notice how others are feeling based on their body language and expressions. This can be done during family outings or even by watching a movie together and discussing the characters' emotions.

- **Empathy Journaling:** Have your child keep a journal where they write about social interactions they've observed. They can reflect on how people interacted, how they think others felt, and how they felt themselves. This helps deepen their understanding of social dynamics.

- **Perspective-Taking Discussions:** After a social situation, discuss it with your child. Ask questions like, "How do you think that person felt?" or "Why do you think they acted that way?" This encourages your child to think beyond their own perspective and consider others' experiences.

---

"If bribery works, is it really so bad? Parenting is just poker with higher stakes—and way more snack breaks."

---

# CHAPTER 6

## REINFORCEMENT FOR BAD BEHAVIOR

There's a term players use for someone who makes reckless decisions but still manages to win—it's called being a "donkey" or "donking." (I actually don't know if this is a universal term or just something they say in my parents poker group.) Regardless, imagine a player going all-in with a 2 and 7 off-suit, one of the worst starting hands in poker. By all logic, this move should lead to a swift loss. But then, by some stroke of luck, the flop reveals a 2, 2, and 7, giving the player an unexpected full house. Suddenly, this reckless decision is rewarded, despite the odds, and the player is encouraged to take similar risks in the future.

This scenario isn't just a poker anomaly; it mirrors a common issue in parenting and life. When bad decisions or undesirable behaviors lead to positive outcomes, they're reinforced, making them more likely to be repeated. This is a key lesson in both poker and parenting: reinforcement, whether positive or negative, shapes future behavior.

In poker, players who "donk" their way to a win often start to believe that risky or illogical strategies will pay off in the long run. This can lead to a pattern of bad decisions, backed by the rare occasions when those decisions were rewarded. In parenting, a similar dynamic occurs when a child's bad behavior is inadvertently reinforced. The child learns that certain actions—like throwing a tantrum or ignoring instructions—can lead to a desired outcome, making them more likely to repeat the behavior.

For example, consider the classic scenario of a child throwing a tantrum in a grocery store, demanding a candy bar. In a moment of desperation, the parent buys the candy to calm the child down and avoid a public scene. The immediate relief for the parent is undeniable—sweet, glorious silence. But the long-term consequence? The child learns that tantrums are an effective strategy for getting what they want. Just like the poker "donkey" who wins a hand with a terrible play, the child's bad behavior is rewarded, reinforcing it for the future.

I've seen this pattern of reinforcement in other areas too. I recall therapeutic conversations with a college student who confessed to being a chronic procrastinator. She would wait until the night before to start a multi-page paper or cram for a test. Despite her last-minute approach, she always managed to pull through with good grades. The lack of immediate consequences for her procrastination only reinforced the behavior. She had no real motivation to change because, in her experience, procrastination worked. Her brain had its own internal slot machine that kept paying out every time she pulled the lever at the very last minute.

The key takeaway here is that when and how you reinforce behavior matters greatly. It's a comforting notion to think that children will behave simply because we expect them to, but the reality is more complex. The most effective way to guide behavior is through immediate reinforcement of appropriate actions. For example, if my child picks up their toys as soon as they're asked, they might get a small reward (bribe), like a handful of marshmallows. For some reason, marshmallows were a magic motivator for my youngest son; he would do almost anything for them! If only adults were as easy to motivate—imagine receiving a box of Ferrero Rochers every time you filed taxes on time.

But what about when your child doesn't do as they're asked or misbehaves? The same principle applies: consequences for inappropriate behavior should be immediate. The sooner a child experiences the outcome of their actions, the stronger the association between behavior and consequence. If there's too much of a delay, the child may not connect the consequence with the behavior, rendering the lesson ineffective.

In both poker and parenting, reinforcement is a powerful tool. Whether you're trying to curb bad behavior or cultivate good habits, the timing and consistency of your responses can make all the difference. As parents, it's our job to be mindful of how our actions—intended or not—might be shaping our children's future behavior.

REFLECTION QUESTIONS:

- Can you think of a time when you unintentionally reinforced a behavior—whether with your child, a colleague, or even yourself? What was the immediate result, and did it snowball into a long-term issue?

- How did you realize that your actions were encouraging the very behavior you wanted to avoid? What was your "aha" moment?

- What specific behavior would you like to change now, and how can you consistently reinforce the actions you want to see instead?

- Have you considered keeping a journal to track progress? How might reflecting on both behavioral shifts and your emotional responses help you stay on course?

# CHAPTER 7

## RECOVERY

### REINFORCE RESILIENCE

I once stumbled across an article online titled, "Revealed: The Single Best Way to Recover From a Bad Beat." Now, as someone who's spent a fair amount of time around poker players, I couldn't resist a peek. The key takeaway? Bad beats are inevitable, but how you recover from them can actually make you a stronger player. One quote from the article stuck with me:

> "Poker is a war of information. If you gather more information than your opponents do, analyze it more carefully than they do, and use it more effectively than they do, in the long run, it is inevitable that you will take their money." — *Robert Woolley*.

This little nugget of wisdom isn't just for the poker table—it's pure gold for parents too. Think about it: as parents, we're constantly gathering information about our children—how they think, how they react, what makes them tick. Just like a seasoned poker player studies their opponents to inform their next move, parents observe and analyze their children to better understand their needs and responses. The better we understand our children, the more effective we can be in guiding them through life's inevitable ups and downs.

When I talk about recovery, I'm referring to how a child bounces back after facing a challenge or setback. This could be anything from a disappointing grade to a spat with a friend or sibling. Just like in poker, where a player has to recover mentally from a bad beat to stay in the game, children must learn how to regain their emotional balance when things go sideways. And just like in poker, this process of recovery is crucial for long-term success—not just in games, but in life.

In another article by Ashley Adams titled "Stud Poker Strategy: Recovery," she breaks down recovery in a way that really resonates:

> "The lessons for me are clear. Recovery takes time, even for thoughtful, good players. Recovery takes intent. Most importantly, recovery takes a willingness to recognize a dangerous situation and one's own imperfections."

This idea of intentional recovery is just as important in parenting. Helping our children recover from setbacks isn't just about making them feel better in the moment; it's about teaching them resilience. It's about guiding them to understand that setbacks are a part of life, and how they respond to those setbacks is what truly defines their character.

For parents, this means being *tuned in* to the signals our children send us, recognizing when they're struggling, and helping them process their emotions in a healthy way. It means providing them with the tools they need to bounce back—whether that's through a heart-to-heart, offering support, or sometimes just giving them the space they need to work through their feelings. It's a bit like handing them a life jacket when they're struggling to stay afloat and reminding them that, yes, they *can* swim to shore.

My daughter is a bit of a perfectionist and when it comes to competing, if she isn't performing well, I can tell. She has this annoyed look that I can see from a mile away and when I see it, I know that we are both about to lose our cool. In poker, a "tell" is a slight change in behavior that other players are observing in order to gather information. My daughter's " tell" is most likely not noticeable to other spectators, but to me, it is incredibly visible. In the midst of the game it is hard for her to realize and recognize her annoyance and change in mood, that we both know is going to impact her performance. At first, I gave her a glare that only a mom can give when they know that their child is acting a fool. I later realized that didn't help, and we talked about giving her a signal to help her realize she needed to shape up and get on the recovery road.

Recovery also involves helping children recognize their own imperfections and the imperfections of the situations they find themselves in. It's about teaching them that it's okay to fail, that it's okay to feel disappointed, and that these experiences are golden opportunities to learn and grow. It's a bit like letting them in on a secret: nobody wins all the time, and that's perfectly fine.

Just as in poker, where a player must get back in the game after a bad beat, children must learn to get back into life after a setback. And just like in poker, where a player's recovery is reinforced by sticking to their strategy and keeping their cool, a child's resilience is reinforced by knowing they have the support and tools to recover.

As parents, we can reinforce recovery by acknowledging the effort it takes, by celebrating the small victories along the way, and by reminding our children that each challenge they overcome makes them stronger and more capable for the next one.

## REINFORCING RECOVERY

In the world of parenting, I often think of recovery as a behavioral turnaround. No child is perfect, and every parent knows that mistakes are just part of the package deal. Our job is to help our children learn from these mistakes, guiding them to regain their emotional balance after a difficult situation, like when they face the consequences of their actions.

The idea of reinforcing recovery by providing an incentive for change is particularly powerful. Let's be real: recovery doesn't always happen on its own. If we want to see real progress, we need to approach it strategically, using the information we've gathered about our children's behavior to create rewards that encourage improvement. You're the coach who knows just what play to call to turn the game around.

In my experience, a reinforced recovery method can be especially effective, particularly when immediate consequences might only make things worse. For some children, simply stating the expected behavior and then incrementally rewarding them as they work their way back to the straight and narrow can be a better approach than going full-on disciplinarian.

Imagine this scenario: a child hits their sibling , and the parent, calmly but firmly, responds by saying, "It's not okay to hit your brother/sister. You're going to lose video game privileges for that behavior for one week. However, if you apologize and manage to keep your hands to yourself, you can earn a day back. For every day that you don't hit, you'll earn back one day off your consequence."

What's happening here? The child experiences the consequence of losing a privilege, which reinforces that the behavior was unacceptable. But—and here's the magic—they're also motivated to change their behavior because they have the opportunity to earn back what was lost. It's a bit like dangling a carrot in front of them, but with the added lesson that good behavior really does pay off. This approach not only helps the child recover from their mistake but also encourages them to develop better habits in the long run. It's like turning a losing hand into a winning one by playing your cards right.

Reinforcing recovery doesn't just help in the short term—it's a long-term strategy for instilling resilience and the ability to bounce back from mistakes. By focusing on this approach, we as parents can guide our children towards positive behavioral changes, making the process of turning around their behavior a rewarding and effective experience.

So the next time your child slips up, think of it as an opportunity for a recovery play. By reinforcing their path back to good behavior, you're not just addressing the issue at hand—you're teaching them that mistakes are part of the game, and with the right moves, they can always come back stronger.

---

"Reward the comeback, don't just punish the mistake."

---

Let's face it—children are going to mess up. But by reinforcing recovery, we show them that getting back on track is not only possible but also worth the effort. And in the grand game of parenting, that's a win-win.

## REINFORCED RECOVERY

Have you ever watched a poker player who's so out-stacked on chips that they look like they're just about ready to throw in the towel? It's as if they've mentally checked out because winning feels about as likely as getting struck by lightning while holding a winning lottery ticket. This same dynamic can happen in parenting, especially with children or teens who feel like they've dug themselves so deep into a hole that climbing out seems impossible.

I once worked with a family whose teenage son had a bit of a rebellious streak—okay, more than a bit. His misbehavior led to a snowball effect of escalating punishments. First, he was grounded for a day, then a week, and before long, he was looking at months of restrictions. It was the parental version of "three strikes, you're out." The teen, feeling like he was in an inescapable pit, would often say, "At this point, I've got nothing left to lose, so why would I bother behaving any differently?" For him, a win—like regaining his freedom or improving his behavior—felt about as likely as convincing a cat to take a bath—It's just not gonna happen.

In situations like this, where a child or teen has lost all motivation to change, it might be time to reshuffle the deck and try a different approach. Enter the *reinforced recovery method*—a strategy designed to stop the downward spiral and give children a way back to positive behavior. Instead of letting them sink deeper into negativity, you offer them incremental opportunities to improve and earn back privileges, piece by piece. They can climb out of this hole they're in, one rung at a time.

For example, imagine if the teen knew that completing specific chores, showing respect, and following house rules could earn him days off his grounding. Instead of staring down a seemingly endless punishment, he'd start to see light at the end of the tunnel. Every respectful action or chore completed would bring him one step closer to freedom. By gradually reducing the length of his grounding based on his behavior, he (or she, girls get grounded too, ya know) begin to realize that change is not only possible but within their control.

Timing, as they say, is everything. The effectiveness of reinforcements or consequences is closely tied to how quickly they follow the behavior in question. When a consequence is applied immediately after a child's inappropriate behavior, the connection between the two is as clear as day. For example, if one sibling hits another and the consequence is handed down right away, the child quickly learns that hitting results in an immediate, unfavorable outcome—no ambiguity, no delay, just a straight shot from action to consequence.

But if a consequence is delayed—whether by minutes, hours, or, heaven forbid, days—the association between the behavior and the consequence gets murky. The child might struggle to connect the dots, wondering why they're suddenly in trouble for something they did ages ago (in child time, that's about five minutes). This can lead to confusion, a sense of injustice, and, worst of all, resentment.

Remember, it's not about avoiding mistakes—it's about how we recover from them. And when we show our children that they can always find a way back, we're teaching them one of life's most valuable lessons: resilience.

## WATCH YOUR "TILT"

In poker, recovery and resilience are essential skills for long-term success. A bad beat—a moment when a strong hand unexpectedly loses—can rattle even the most experienced player. However, top players understand that these setbacks are part of the game. Instead of dwelling on the loss, they quickly refocus, analyze what went wrong, and adjust their strategy for the next hand.

---

*Resilience in poker means not letting a single loss affect your overall mindset or decision-making process.*

---

Practical recovery involves taking a deep breath, reassessing the table dynamics, and continuing to play with discipline and patience. Players like Daniel Negreanu emphasize the importance of maintaining emotional control and not going on "tilt"—a state where emotions dictate play, often leading to more losses. By staying resilient, poker players turn setbacks into learning opportunities, ensuring that one bad hand doesn't spiral into a losing streak.

## SUMMARY OF LESSONS LEARNED

This chapter emphasizes the importance of recovery and resilience, both in poker and parenting. Just as poker players must bounce back from a bad beat to stay in the game, children must learn to recover emotionally and behaviorally after setbacks. The chapter highlights the concept of *reinforced recovery,* where children are given opportunities to earn back privileges by demonstrating positive behavior. This approach not only helps them regain their footing but also teaches them that change and improvement are within their control. The timing of reinforcements and consequences is crucial, as immediate feedback strengthens the connection between actions and outcomes, promoting better decision-making and resilience.

## HOMEWORK

Reflect on a recent situation where your child or someone in your life faced a setback or displayed undesirable behavior. How did you respond? Consider how you might apply the reinforced recovery method. Identify specific actions or behaviors that could help them regain lost privileges or improve their situation. Over the next week, implement this strategy, offering immediate feedback and small rewards for positive behavior. Keep track of any changes and reflect on how this approach affects their motivation and resilience. What did you learn about the power of reinforcement in shaping behavior? How might you continue to use these techniques in the future?

# CHAPTER 8

## FIRE THE WARNING SHOT

In poker, when you "raise," you're upping the ante, telling everyone at the table, "I've got something good, and I'm not afraid to back it up." When you make a second or subsequent raise, known as a "re-raise," you're *really* turning up the heat—essentially saying, "I'm serious, and you'd better think twice before you call." These actions serve as a kind of warning shot, signaling to other players, "I've got a strong hand, and I'm giving you a heads-up."

In parenting, firing a "warning shot" before imposing a consequence works much the same way. It's a heads-up to your child: "You've crossed a line, and if this behavior continues, there will be consequences." This approach helps them fully grasp the potential repercussions of their actions and gives them a chance to *correct* their behavior before things escalate to the dreaded punishment stage.

Firing that warning shot is essential. It ensures your child is aware of both the expectations and the consequences if those expectations aren't met. This way, if they continue with the inappropriate behavior, it's harder for them to be upset with you—after all, they were given a fair chance to change course.

Children don't always realize when their behavior needs to

change. They might be so caught up in their own world that they don't see the storm clouds gathering on the horizon. By giving a warning, you're not just setting clear boundaries but also offering them an opportunity to make a better decision. Without that warning, the punishment can feel abrupt and unjust, leading to frustration and resentment—basically, a full-blown meltdown over something that could have been easily avoided. The warning shot serves as an educational tool, putting the decision-making power in the child's hands and allowing them to take responsibility for their actions. It's an important step in their behavioral and emotional development, helping them understand that they have control over their decisions and the outcomes that follow.

Now, while it's important to set a clear behavioral standard in the home (because let's face it, we're not running a circus here), it's equally important to provide opportunities for learning. That's why I often use the phrase "prepare for punishment." This isn't a threat from Judge Judy; it's a heads-up. It means you've acknowledged the inappropriate behavior and are giving your child advance notice of a potential consequence if they continue down the same path. "Storm's coming, childdo, might want to grab an umbrella—or, you know, stop the tantrum."

The ultimate goal, of course, is for our children to learn to adjust their behavior on their own, ideally before we have to step in with the threat. The key is to make it crystal clear *why* the consequence is happening so that your child can make the connection between their behavior and the result.


THE IMPORTANCE OF WARNING SHOTS

If your child misses their midnight curfew, you might tell them, "If you're late again, I'll take away your cell phone privilege. For every ten minutes you're late, that's one day without your cell phone." Now, they know the deal. If they come waltzing in thirty minutes late, they can't exactly claim ignorance when you collect their phone for three days. It's crucial to be specific about the consequences so that your child knows exactly what to expect if they repeat the behavior. This way, when the punishment comes, they're less likely to argue that it's unfair—because, well, they saw it coming from a mile away.

When your child is late, you can calmly remind them, "Remember, we agreed that being thirty minutes late would mean three days without your phone. You made the choice to stay out, and now you've got to face the music." In the realm of poker, a player clearly states how much they want to raise, so the other players know exactly what's expected of them if they want to stay in the game. With clearly stated expectations, both players and children are more likely to respond accordingly.

So, what specific consequences have you implemented with your children? Did you find that accountability improved when your child couldn't argue with a "predetermined punishment"? It's amazing how quickly things smooth out when everyone knows the rules and what's at stake—whether you're at the poker table or the dinner table.

At the end of the day, setting expectations and consequences isn't just about keeping order; it's about teaching our children that their choices have predictable outcomes. And isn't that one of the most valuable life lessons we can give them?

## RAISING, RE-RAISING, AND FIRING WARNING SHOTS: THE POKER PLAYBOOK FOR PARENTING (AND LIFE)

In poker, the tactics of raising, re-raising, and firing a warning shot are more than just ways to beef up the pot—they're crucial strategies used to assert dominance, gauge opponents, and *control the game.* When a player raises, they are increasing the bet, signaling confidence in their hand. This move not only ups the ante but also puts pressure on other players to either match the bet or fold. A raise is a way of saying, "I've got something good, and I'm backing it up."

A re-raise, which occurs when a player increases the bet after someone else has already raised, turns up the heat even more. It's a bold statement, often used to test an opponent's resolve or to push them out of the hand. The re-raise acts as a warning shot, letting others know that the player is serious and that continuing could be costly.

But here's the kicker—these strategies aren't just about the cards. They're about reading your opponents, getting inside their heads, and forcing them into tough decisions. A well-timed raise or re-raise can make even the most confident player second-guess their hand. It's psychological warfare at its finest, where the real power lies not in the cards themselves, but in how you play them. Mastering these tactics allows poker players to seize control of the game, manipulating the flow of bets and steering the outcome in their favor like a maestro conducting a high-stakes symphony. Whether you're at the poker table, the negotiating table, or the dinner table with your children, the principles remain the same. Raising the stakes, re-raising to apply pressure, and giving that well-timed warning shot are all about setting the tone, asserting control, and influencing the decisions of others. It's about knowing when to push, when to pull back, and when to play your cards close to the vest.

## HOMEWORK

Reflect on your current approach to discipline. Consider how often you give your child a warning before enforcing a consequence. Think of a recent situation where your child's behavior needed correction. Did you give them a chance to adjust their actions before imposing a punishment?

This week, practice firing a "warning shot" in situations where your child's behavior is heading in the wrong direction. Clearly communicate the expected behavior and the specific consequences if the behavior continues. For example, if your child is at risk of losing a privilege, explain exactly what they need to do to avoid that outcome. Afterward, reflect on the effectiveness of this approach. Did it help your child make better choices? How did it impact your relationship and their understanding of accountability? Take notes on the outcomes and consider discussing these experiences with your partner or a fellow parent. How can you continue to refine your use of warning shots to foster a better understanding of consequences and decision-making in your child?

# CHAPTER 9

## THE SHOWDOWN

In poker, a "showdown" happens after all the bets are in, and the final two players lay their cards on the table to see who takes home the pot. It's the ultimate moment of truth, where the bluffing stops, and the cards do the talking. The term "showdown" often brings to mind images of old western movies, where two cowboys, with pistols at the ready, face off in a duel, with the survivor emerging as the victor.

Professional poker players approach this showdown with calculated strategies, understanding that this is the final moment to reveal their hand and claim the pot:

**Value Betting:** In poker, value betting is when a player bets on a strong hand to extract maximum value from their opponent. It's like saying, "I know I've got the goods, so let's see how much I can get out of you." In parenting, value betting might look like strategically picking your battles. You know your child has a "strong hand" when they're well-behaved or doing something right, so you "bet" on them by praising their good behavior or rewarding them with something they value. The goal? To reinforce those positive actions and get the most out of those good behavior moments.

**Bluff Catching:** Then there's bluff catching, where a player with a medium-strength hand calls a bet, suspecting their opponent is bluffing. In the parenting world, this is all about calling your child's bluff when they try to pull a fast one on you. You know the scenario: your child insists they're "too sick" to go to school, but you've seen this bluff before—usually when there's a test or a less-than-fun activity involved. Bluff catching in parenting is about reading between the lines and knowing when your little one is trying to outsmart you. It's a tricky dance of suspicion and experience, but when you catch that bluff, it's a small yet satisfying victory.

**Information Gathering:** The showdown is also prime time for gathering intel on your opponents. Poker players watch closely to see how others play strong vs. weak hands, picking up on tells and tendencies they can exploit in future rounds. As a parent, this might look like noticing your child's patterns—how they react when they're tired, hungry, or just in need of attention. By understanding these tendencies, you can better navigate future "showdowns" and maybe even head off a tantrum before it hits full steam. After all, knowing is half the battle, and having that parental sixth sense can save the day (and your sanity).

**Slow Playing:** Finally, there's the art of slow playing— underplaying a strong hand earlier in the game to lure opponents into betting more, only to reveal your strength at the showdown. In parenting, slow playing might be like keeping a cool head while your child is pushing boundaries, waiting for just the right moment to lay down the law. It's about not showing all your cards too soon, letting your child think they've got the upper hand, only to reveal that, yes, you were paying attention all along and, no, they can't have that extra cookie because they didn't finish their dinner. It's the classic, "I was letting you think you were getting away with it, but I've had your number the whole time."

Now, let's bring that tension into the family living room, where a different kind of showdown can unfold between parent and child. It might not involve spurs and six-shooters, value betting and bluff catching, but it can feel just as high-stakes. This is when both sides dig in their heels, refusing to budge. Emotions run high, and it's a battle of wills: Who will emerge victorious? And, more importantly, what does "winning" even mean in this context?

In poker, the winner walks away with the pot—a clear, tangible reward for their skill, strategy, and maybe a little luck. But in parenting, the concept of a "win" is way murkier. When you're in the heat of a parent-child clash, it might feel like the winner is simply the one who gets their way. Maybe it's the parent enforcing a rule or the child resisting bedtime for the 100th time this week.

For a parent, the immediate goal might be to lay down the law, asserting authority to make sure the rules are followed. But what if in doing so, the child feels completely overpowered and unheard? Sure, the parent might win the battle, but what's the cost? Losing the trust and cooperation of your child can be a steep price to pay. On the flip side, if the child wins by getting their way, it can chip away at the parent's authority and set the stage for even more intense showdowns down the road.

In parenting, the stakes are higher than in any poker game, and the rewards are often intangible. The real victory in a parent-child showdown isn't about who walks away with the metaphorical win; it's about finding a resolution that fosters positive behavior, mutual respect, and a healthy relationship. The goal isn't to win the moment but to win the long game—raising children who feel valued, understood, and willing to work with you rather than against you.

Just like a seasoned poker player, parents need to think *strategically* about how to handle these conflicts. Sometimes that means knowing when to fold 'em—stepping back from the standoff and finding a middle ground. Maybe it's turning the clash into a teachable moment, where both sides can cool off and come back to the table with a better understanding of each other. It's not about one person walking away with all the chips, but about everyone walking away feeling like they've gained something valuable.

The true victory in these family showdowns lies in navigating the conflicts with wisdom and care, ensuring that both parent and child emerge with a deeper understanding of each other and a stronger bond. Because at the end of the day, it's not about winning the pot— it's about building a relationship that stands the test of time.

## WHAT DO YOU THINK CONSTITUTES A WIN FOR A PARENT? WHAT DO YOU THINK CONSTITUTES A WIN FOR A CHILD?

At first glance, the obvious answer might be that either the parent or the child gets what they want out of the conflict, while the other is left to lick their wounds and accept defeat. But as anyone who's ever tried to negotiate with a toddler (or a teenager, for that matter) knows, the concept of "winning" is a bit more nuanced when it comes to parenting. It's not just about getting your way; it's about meeting your parental goals.

*So, what exactly are your parenting goals?*

Maybe it's ensuring that your children feel unconditionally loved, teaching them to be kind, or simply getting them to behave appropriately without losing your sanity. These goals are a far cry from those of a poker player, who's more focused on strategizing their way to a big payday. But if I were a betting person (which, you know, I am!) I'd wager that beyond just winning the pot, a poker player also aims to earn respect from their peers—a respect that's earned through consistent performance and a knack for knowing when to hold 'em and when to fold 'em.

In that sense, parenting and poker aren't so different. Just as a seasoned poker player earns the esteem of their fellow players by consistently making smart moves, parents seek to earn the respect of their children through consistent, thoughtful, and fair parenting. So then, how do you earn the respect of your children? It's not by having the best hand every time (because let's face it, no parent does), but by consistently performing well when it matters most.

But what does it mean to "perform well" as a parent? It's about being fair, setting clear boundaries, following through on consequences, and showing your children that while you might not always have the easiest hand to play, you're going to play it with integrity. If you're consistent in this, over time, your children will learn to respect you—not because you always "win," but because you always show up and do your best.

Consider a scenario where a teenager comes to you with a well-thought-out argument, complete with supporting evidence, to secure a later curfew. If they've done their homework and "play their cards right," they might just win the showdown. And honestly, if they've gone to that much effort, maybe they've earned it.

On the flip side, picture a showdown with a toddler. You've told them it's time for a nap, and they're refusing with every ounce of their tiny being. You might have to carry them to their room, kicking and screaming all the way, but if you enforce that nap time, you've won the showdown—at least for now. (Let's not even get into the sequel that will happen when they refuse to get out of bed.)

I once had an epic showdown with my oldest son when he was 7, right outside daycare. He had used his tablet to break an air vent in my car. I told him that because he was disrespectful to both his property (the tablet) and mine (the car), he wouldn't be allowed to take his tablet to daycare that day. The showdown was on. He wanted his tablet; I wanted to teach him a lesson. He pleaded, embarrassed both himself and me in front of the daycare staff, clung to me like a barnacle so I couldn't leave, and even pulled out the big guns by threatening not to hug me when I left. He followed me outside, hyperventilating until he gagged. If his secondary goal was to make me feel like the worst parent in the world, mission accomplished. But his primary goal of getting that tablet back? Not so much. I knew better than to let his five-alarm panic attack get the best of me. I walked out, looked at his crying little face through the window, and left. I won the showdown—but wow, was it a hard-fought victory.

*Do you recall any epic showdowns with your children?*

*Did you walk away with the win, or did they outmaneuver you?*

*What caused the clash, and how did you handle it? And more importantly, what did you both learn from the experience?*

## THE ART OF THE SHOWDOWN: A PARENTING CHALLENGE

Over the next week, I've got a little challenge for you: pay close attention to how you handle conflicts with your child. Think of it as your own personal parenting experiment—a chance to see how well you manage those inevitable showdowns without losing your cool (or your sanity). Your mission, should you choose to accept it, is to focus on being consistent in your approach, clearly communicating your expectations, and outlining any consequences ahead of time. When the showdown occurs—and trust me, it will—take a step back and ask yourself a critical question: Is it more important to "win" this moment, or would it be better to find a resolution that benefits your child's long-term development? Because let's face it, while the sweet taste of victory is tempting, sometimes it's more about the big picture than the immediate win.

Once the dust has settled and the house is (hopefully) quiet again, take a few minutes to reflect on the experience. Did you feel like you came out on top, or did your child manage to pull a fast one on you? Did they use their *Puss in Boots* face and emotional fireworks to outmaneuver you? What could you have done differently to turn the situation into a learning opportunity for both of you? And most importantly, how can you apply these insights to future conflicts so you can navigate the delicate balance of authority and empathy like a parenting ninja? Writing down your thoughts after these encounters isn't just a great way to vent (though that's definitely a bonus)—it's a chance to learn and grow as a parent. By reflecting on what worked and what didn't, you can start to see patterns, tweak your strategies, and maybe even avoid some of those showdowns altogether.

Ready, set, parent!

# CHAPTER 10

## TABLE TALK

Despite the many similarities between poker and parenting, there are some significant differences—especially when it comes to *communication*. In poker, communication is more about being cagey, and keeping your cards close to your chest, while in parenting, communication is about transparency and laying the cards all out on the table.

As a parent, my goal is to communicate openly and transparently with my child. I want them to know when I'm proud of them, and—let's be honest—when they're driving me up the wall. Clear communication helps us understand what we expect of one another, and it builds a foundation of trust and mutual respect. It's like saying, "Hey, we're in this game together, and I want to make sure we're both on the same page."

But in poker, communication is an entirely different ballgame. Players aim to be as cryptic as possible, their faces unreadable, their intentions hidden. In the world of poker, good communication is all about concealing your thoughts and keeping your strategies secret. It's like walking through a verbal minefield where saying too much could cost you the game.

## "TABLE TALK" IN POKER VS. PARENTING:

"Table talk" in poker is a tactic used to manipulate or unsettle opponents. A player might throw out a line like, "Are you sure you want to bet on that hand?" or "You really should fold before things get ugly." It's part bluff, part psychology, and all about gaining the upper hand. The aim is to create doubt, throw opponents off their game, or even bait them into making a mistake. Some players use it to fish for information, while others use it to intimidate. Either way, it's a game of wits where communication is more about misdirection than clarity.

As a parent, though, I'm aiming for the opposite of poker's table talk. I'm not trying to bluff my way through a conversation with my child or trick them into compliance. Instead, I'm focused on being as clear as possible. I want them to know exactly where I stand, what I expect, and why certain rules are in place. This kind of open, honest dialogue is crucial for building a healthy relationship where both parent and child feel understood and respected.

## REFLECTIONS ON COMMUNICATION STYLES:

Now, let's take a moment to think back to our own childhoods.

*What was your communication style like with your parents?* Were they open and transparent, or was communication more like a poker game, with each side trying to guess what the other was really thinking? *What did you appreciate about the way they communicated with you, and what do you wish had been different?*

In many ways, the way we were communicated with as children influences how we communicate with our own children. If our parents were more reserved or strategic in their communication, we might find ourselves echoing that style without even realizing it. But should our communication with our children be a mirror of how we were raised, or should we strive for something different? And what about how we communicate with other adults—should that change when we're talking to children?

> *"The best hand a parent has is a clear and honest conversation."*

If we were to talk to adults the way we sometimes talk to our children, like saying, "Put down that phone right now, mister!" to your boss or "You're not getting dessert until you finish your broccoli" to a dinner date. You'd probably be met with a mix of confusion and a quick exit—or worse, a stern lecture about workplace etiquette. The reality is, we often use a tone with our children that would be considered downright rude if we used it with anyone over four feet tall.

This begs the question: *Can we communicate with our children in a way that keeps us in charge without sounding like we're auditioning for a role as the villain in a children' movie?*

Spoiler alert: *Yes, we can!* But it takes a bit of finesse and a good dose of intentionality.

## THE POLITENESS PARADOX

I'll admit, I'm guilty of sometimes skipping the basic courtesies with my children that I'd never dream of neglecting when talking to another adult. For instance, before my youngest son turned one, I found myself frequently enlisting my older two for quick tasks. "Go grab me a diaper," or "Give him a toy," I'd say. It was straight to the point, no frills, and certainly no "please" or "thank you." But if I'm being honest, I wouldn't dream of talking to a co-worker that way—unless I was really angling for an HR intervention.

Why the double standard? Is it because I'm in a position of power that I feel it's okay to skip the polite phrasing? Or is it simply because I expect my children to do as they're told? Either way, if I want to raise children who communicate respectfully, it might be time to practice what I preach.

Communication styles really get put to the test when there's a disagreement—much like in poker. Imagine a poker player folding a pre-flop hand of an off-suit 7 and 2 because the odds of winning with such a hand are slim. Sensible, right? Now, picture another player who thinks outside the box, maybe even my father, who loved playing that exact hand because, as he'd say, "No one expects a call on it." It's a risky move, but it's all part of his strategy.

So, how do you think that difference in strategy would be communicated at the table? It's a delicate dance of asserting one's opinion while respecting the other's approach. Poker players have to navigate these differences with a blend of confidence and tact. They might needle each other a bit, but at the end of the day, it's about respect for the game and the players.

Similarly, as parents, we need to find that balance between authority and respect when communicating with our children. Sure, we're in charge, but that doesn't mean we should drop the "please" and "thank yous" just because we're talking to someone a few feet shorter than us. Modeling the behavior we want to see—even in the smallest interactions—is key.

This doesn't mean we're letting go of our authority. It just means we're showing our children that you can be in charge and still be respectful. It's about making sure they feel valued and heard, even when they're not the ones calling the shots.

So next time you're about to bark out a command—er, request—take a second to consider how you'd say it if you were talking to an adult. Would you add a "please" or a "thank you"? Would you frame it as a request rather than an order? And when disagreements arise, think about how you'd handle it if you were at a poker table: with a mix of confidence, tact, and respect.

In the grand poker game of parenting, the cards you play matter, but so does how you play them. By modeling respectful communication, you're teaching your children that authority and kindness aren't mutually exclusive. After all, the way we handle our "hands" at the parenting table speaks volumes about the kind of relationships we want to build.

By using language that acknowledges your child's feelings and explains the reasoning behind your requests, you're not just maintaining control—you're teaching them how to navigate the world with respect and understanding. And who knows? Maybe one day, they'll thank you for treating them like a person instead of a tiny, unreasonable dictator.

So next time you're about to drop the hammer with a stern "No more screen time!" consider rephrasing it. Try something like, "I know you love playing that game, but let's take a break so you can focus on something else for a bit." It might not be as satisfying as an authoritative decree, but it'll definitely score you points in the long game of parenting—and keep you from sounding like the bad guy in your own house.

---

"If poker players can be polite while trying to take each other's money, surely we can say 'please' when asking for a diaper."

---

So, go ahead—shuffle up, deal with respect, and watch how your communication game changes for the better.

## EXERCISE: THE BALANCE OF RESPECT AND COMMUNICATION

Let's have some fun with finding the sweet spot between being the boss and not sounding like a drill sergeant. We're going to list 20 situations where explaining your decision to your child is necessary. Think of it as the ultimate parenting challenge—how do you lay down the law without turning into a dictator? For each scenario, come up with a way to explain your reasoning that respects your child's feelings but still leaves no doubt that you're the one in charge.

### Curfew Time
*Explanation:* "I know staying out later sounds fun, but we've

set your curfew at midnight to ensure you're safe when the roads are less busy and we know where you are. Plus, let's be real—nothing good happens after midnight except reruns of infomercials."

### Limiting Screen Time

*Explanation:* "I understand you love playing games, but we limit screen time to make sure you have time for other activities that are important for your growth and less harmful to your eyes."

### Homework Before Play

*Explanation:* "I get that you want to play right now, but finishing your homework first helps you stay on track and enjoy your free time without any worries."

### Healthy Eating

*Explanation:* "I know you'd prefer pizza for dinner, but eating vegetables is important for staying healthy and strong, which helps you do all the fun things you love. Plus, who knows? You might develop X-ray vision. (Okay, maybe not, but still!)"

### Bedtime Routine

*Explanation:* "I understand staying up late feels more exciting, but a consistent bedtime helps you get the rest you need to feel good and do your best in school."

### Chores on the Weekend

*Explanation:* "I know you'd rather relax, but doing your chores helps keep the house clean for everyone, and we all need to pitch in.

Plus, it's good practice for when you're a famous rock star and need to clean your tour bus!"

### No Phone During Meals

*Explanation*: "I understand you want to check your phone, but mealtimes are for family connection. We'll have more time to talk and enjoy each other's company without distractions."

### Sharing Toys with Siblings

*Explanation*: "I get that it's hard to share, but taking turns with your siblings teaches everyone to play fair and helps avoid conflicts."

### Why They Can't Have a Pet

*Explanation*: "I know you want a pet, but pets are a big responsibility. Right now, our schedule doesn't allow us to give a pet the attention it needs."

### Going to a Party

*Explanation*: "I know you want to go to that party, but it's a school night, and we both know that you're not getting up for class tomorrow"

### Why They Have to Go to School

*Explanation*: "I know school isn't always fun, but it's important for your future. It helps you learn new things and prepares you for what you want to do later in life."

### Why They Can't Watch a Certain Movie

*Explanation:* "I understand you want to see that movie, but it's rated for adults, and some parts might be too scary or confusing for you right now. Plus, nightmares are not a good look—trust me."

### Why They Can't Buy Expensive Items
*Explanation:* "I know you really want that toy, but it's expensive, and we have to save money for other important things, too—like snacks and surprise ice cream trips. Priorities, right?"

### Why You're Limiting Their Candy Intake
*Explanation:* "I understand you want more candy, but too much sugar can make you feel sick and isn't good for your teeth."

### Why They Can't Go Out Without Adult Supervision
*Explanation:* "I know you feel grown up, but you're still young, and it's our job to make sure you're safe. We'll need to go with you or find another trusted adult to be there."

### Why They Can't Skip Family Events
*Explanation:* "I understand you might find family events boring, but they're important for building relationships and staying connected with our family. Plus, there's always a chance of cake. Cake makes everything better."

### Why They Have to Save Money
*Explanation:* "I know you want to spend your allowance right away, but saving helps you buy something bigger and more meaningful later on."

. . .

### Why They Have to Go to the Dentist

*Explanation:* "I understand you don't like the dentist, but it's important for keeping your teeth healthy so you can avoid pain and problems in the future."

### Why They Need to Say Please and Thank You

*Explanation:* "I know it might seem like just words, but saying 'please' and 'thank you' shows good manners and makes people more likely to help you out."

### Why You're Setting a Limit on Social Media

*Explanation:* "I understand you enjoy social media, but too much time online can affect your mood and sleep. We set limits to help you stay balanced and healthy—plus, less screen time means more time for real-life adventures. Like, you know, reading a book or actually spending time with your friends, OUTSIDE!"

## Reflection:

After completing this exercise, take a moment to reflect on how these explanations might change the way your child perceives your decisions. Consider how this approach can help foster respect and understanding in your relationship, and think about how you can incorporate this style of communication into your everyday interactions.

### THE BALANCE OF RESPECT AND COMMUNICATION

Is respect only earned when people do exactly what you want? When you think about your relationships with other adults, do you always need to be on the same page for the relationship to be respectful? Hopefully not, because if that were the case, we'd all be living in constant disagreement limbo! My hope is that respect can thrive even in the midst of differing opinions, whether you're dealing with another adult or your child. The secret sauce lies in how you communicate those differences.

Have you ever heard the phrase, "agree to disagree"? It's the Switzerland of phrases—neutral, peaceful, and ready to maintain the relationship despite the disagreement.

Validation is like the VIP pass in communication. It acknowledges the other person's perspective as legitimate, even if you're seeing things from a different angle. By validating someone else's opinion, you're basically saying, "Hey, more than one viewpoint can exist here, and that's okay." This reduces the pressure for one person to be right and the other wrong, making room for a more balanced and respectful exchange.

But let's be real—sometimes validation alone doesn't cut it, especially with children. They often need more than just a nod to their feelings; they need to understand the "why" behind your decisions. For example, you might say, "I get that an early curfew feels unfair, and I know a later curfew would let you hang out with your friends longer. But your father and I have set a midnight curfew to make sure you're home before the bars close and the roads get riskier."

In this scenario, giving an explanation helps your child see that your decision wasn't made to ruin their social life. It shows them that you're thinking about their safety, which helps them feel respected even when they don't get their way. Plus, it reinforces that as a parent, you're making decisions with their best interests at heart.

## KEEP IT SHORT AND SWEET

Now, while explanations are important, let's not turn them into a TED Talk. Keep it clear and concise. There's no need to exhaust yourself with a monologue, especially if your child has already made up their mind about how they feel. Children, much like poker players, don't want a 30-minute explanation for why you made the decision you did. They want the CliffNotes version.

I like to use the saying, "state an expectation, not a long explanation." Instead of going into a drawn-out reasoning session, you might simply say, "You can't stay out past midnight because nothing good happens after midnight. I'll be worried the entire time you're gone, and you need to get up early tomorrow." Short, to the point, and hard to argue with.

By striking a balance between respect, validation, and concise communication, you can maintain your parental authority while fostering mutual respect in your relationships with both adults and children. It's about making sure everyone at the table—whether in poker or in your family—feels heard, valued, and understood, even when the final decision doesn't go their way.

## BALANCING COMMUNICATION: CLARITY AND AUTHORITY IN PARENTING

As parents, striking the right balance between providing information and maintaining authority is a delicate dance. You want your child to understand the reasoning behind your decisions, but you don't want to open Pandora's box of debates. Too much explanation can give a child the impression that they have the right to negotiate or challenge every decision, turning your firm "no" into a never-ending back-and-forth.

Take, for instance, previously stated classic curfew debate: When you said, "Nothing good happens after midnight," and suddenly you're knee-deep in an argument you never signed up for. Your child counters with, "You worry too much. So-and-so's parents let them stay out till 1 a.m.!" The more you explain, the more they dig in their heels, feeling like they need to defend their position. Suddenly, you're playing the role of the defense attorney in the case of *The People vs. A Reasonable Bedtime.*

In poker, clear communication is non-negotiable. The dealer

needs to know exactly what the player intends, whether through a verbal cue like "I raise" or a non-verbal action like pushing chips forward. If a player is unclear—saying one thing while doing another—it causes confusion and can even lead to disputes. Imagine telling your dealer you're folding while at the same time stacking your chips like you're going all in. That's a recipe for some serious table tension!

Similarly, when communicating with your child, clarity is essential. Let's be real—children aren't as compliant as poker dealers. They're more likely to challenge, interpret, and question your words, especially if they sense any ambiguity. If you tell your child, "You need to be headed home by midnight," and they stroll in at 12:30, you're likely to hear, "But you said headed home, not in by midnight." Cue the argument you were hoping to avoid.

One common communication pitfall parents fall into is being unclear about timelines. How many times have you said, "I'll be there in a second," when you know full well it'll be more like ten minutes? Depending on your child's age, they might take that "second" quite literally, and the next thing you know, they're standing next to you asking, "Are you coming yet?" every thirty seconds. By the third or fourth time, both your patience and theirs are wearing thin.

I've been guilty of this myself. So, I've started setting alarms on my phone as a way to keep myself accountable. If I tell my children I need five minutes to finish something, I set a five-minute alarm. When it goes off, we all know it's time to move on to the next thing. It's a simple strategy, but it helps to clear up misunderstandings and reduce the number of times I hear, "But you said...!"

Another tip: Make it clear when something is a *non-negotiable* command versus a casual request. Instead of saying, "Will you clean up your room?" which leaves room for a "no," try, "I need you to clean up your room." This way, your child knows it's not an option. I'm all for giving children choices, but let's not make the mistake of offering a choice where there shouldn't be one.

So, what about you? Do any of these communication hiccups sound familiar? Maybe you've found yourself locked in a curfew debate, or maybe you've inadvertently offered an option where there wasn't supposed to be one. Reflect on these moments and think about how you can tweak your communication style to be clearer and more authoritative, while still being kind and respectful.

*"Clear communication is the bridge that turns intentions into understanding."*

Remember, the goal is to create a balance where your child feels respected and understood, but also knows that when you set an expectation, it's non-negotiable. It's all part of the delicate art of parenting—and much like a poker game, the better your strategy, the smoother the game will go.

## CLARITY IN COMMUNICATION: SETTING EXPECTATIONS

Clear communication is the cornerstone of any successful relationship, whether it's between an employer and employee or a parent and child. Just as an employer has to outline an employee's duties to ensure the job gets done right, parents need to be crystal clear about what they expect from their children. Otherwise, you're setting yourself up for a world of miscommunication—and, let's be honest, some unpleasant arguments.

I vividly remember my mother's infamous "to-do" lists. Every time she went to work, she'd leave us children with a list that might as well have been the length of a novel. One of the regular items was "clean the kitchen." Now, to my young mind, that meant cleaning up after meals and wiping down the counters. Easy enough, right? Wrong. My mother's version of "clean the kitchen" was a full-scale operation: dishes washed and put away, floors swept, appliances wiped down, and probably a small renovation on the side. Needless to say, we often found ourselves in heated debates, arguing that we "didn't know" what she meant. And while our defense rarely worked, it highlighted a critical point: when expectations aren't clearly communicated, arguments are almost inevitable.

The same holds true for behavioral expectations. Telling your child to be home "early" is like telling them to "just bring me something nice" from the store—it's vague, and open to interpretation, For a parent, "early" might mean 9:00 PM, but to a teenager, "early" could very well be a minute before midnight. If you want to avoid that kind of conflict, it's crucial to spell out exactly what you mean. Repeat it, rephrase it, and make sure everyone is on the same page. The clearer you are, the fewer battles you'll face.

Of course, children aren't the only ones who struggle with clarity. Let's be real—parents are guilty of it too. How many times have you said, "I don't know, we'll see," when you're just avoiding a potential meltdown? Or how about the classic, "We'll talk about it later," which is basically parent code for, "I'm not dealing with this right now"? The problem with these vague responses is that children have memories like steel traps. They'll come back at you days later with, "But you said we'd talk about it!" And guess what? Now you're cornered.

Then there's the dreaded, "in a minute." This phrase has to be one of the most misleading in the parental lexicon. When my children hear "in a minute," they think it means sixty seconds. When I say it, I mean, "when I'm free, which could be anywhere from five minutes to sometime next week." The result? A frustrated child who feels like they're being ignored. To remedy this, I'm going back to the phone alarm tip I mentioned earlier. If I say I'll be ready in five minutes, I set a timer for exactly that. When it goes off, we all hear it, and it signals that it's time to follow through. Not only does this help manage expectations, but it also builds trust between my children and me—they know I'm going to keep my word.

Being clear and specific in your communication does wonders for your relationship with your children. It sets clear expectations, minimizes misunderstandings, and, most importantly, shows your children that you respect them enough to be honest and upfront. Plus, it saves you from those dreaded "but you said" moments, which, let's be honest, no one enjoys.

So, the next time you're tempted to give a vague answer or

## LEAHA HAMMER

assume your child knows what you mean, take a moment to spell it out. Trust me, your future self will thank you.

### HOMEWORK

Oh, I'm sorry—did you not expect this book to come with homework? Oops, I guess the blurb wasn't clear enough. Get it?

- **Reflect on Your Communication Habits:** Take a moment to think about your go-to responses when communicating with your child. Do you often throw out vague phrases like "in a minute" or "we'll see"? Spoiler alert: that's code for "probably not, but I'm buying time." Jot down a few examples from recent interactions where your language might have been as clear as a foggy windshield.

- **Clarify Your Expectations:** Pick one or two common scenarios where you and your child end up in a battle of wills. Maybe it's curfew times, chores, or screen time negotiations. Rephrase your expectations to be more specific and write them down. Bonus points if you make them teenager-proof! (Those buggers are smart, THANKS internet!)

- **Practice Setting Boundaries:** This week, challenge yourself to set clear, non-negotiable expectations with your child. Instead of saying, "Can you clean your room?" try, "I need you to clean your room before dinner." Afterward, pat yourself on the back and reflect on how your child responded. Did they actually do it?

- **Use the Alarm Trick:** If you're guilty of saying "in a minute" and then conveniently forgetting, it's time to make use of some tech. Set a timer for exactly when you plan to follow through on what you've promised. Pay attention to how your child reacts—do they stop asking every 30 seconds? And notice if it reduces your stress level, too. Because let's be honest, we could all use a little less nagging, I mean... stress. Sorry, children.

- **Journal Your Progress:** At the end of the week, grab your journal (or the nearest napkin) and reflect on how your communication efforts have impacted your relationship with your child. Did being clearer and more specific cut down on the misunderstandings? How did it affect your child's behavior and your overall sanity? Write it all down—this is your victory lap!

By completing these exercises, you'll not only improve your communication with your child but also foster a stronger, more respectful relationship where both sides feel heard and understood.

# CHAPTER 11

## THE FAMILY POT

In poker, a family pot occurs when every player decides to stay in the hand, suggesting a shared confidence that something good is going to come out of it. It's a scenario where everyone's on board, all chips in, hoping for that big win. Now, take that image and swap out the poker table for your dining room table, and you've got the dynamics of a family working together, everyone committed to a shared goal, confident that their efforts will lead to a positive outcome.

I first stumbled upon the idea of using poker chips as a behavior modification tool from a former supervisor. The concept immediately grabbed my attention—using poker chips as a stand-in for rewards seemed both fun and practical. Let's face it, money talks, especially when it comes to getting children to do things they'd rather not, like doing chores or eating greens. We've all been there—offering up a shiny $10 bill to entice our children to clean the garage or wash the car. But there's a hitch. What happens when you realize you don't have cash on hand when the job's done? The children are left hanging, and the impact of that reward is lost in the delay.

This is where the poker chips come in. Instead of promising cash you may or may not have at the moment, you can hand over poker chips immediately, reinforcing the connection between the work and the reward. Behavior modification, after all, is all about that instant feedback—do the thing, get the reward. And let's be honest, a jar of colorful poker chips is a lot more fun (and visually satisfying) than a promise of cash to come.

The beauty of the chip system is that it acts like a savings account for children. Think about it: children, like adults, often feel the itch to spend money as soon as they get it. But we all know that blowing your earnings on candy bars and dollar store toys isn't exactly the path to financial wisdom. By using poker chips, which need to be accumulated before they can be cashed in, children learn the value of saving up for something they really want.

Take my oldest son, for example. When he was seven, he was obsessed with Transformers. The price range for these toys was broad —anywhere from a couple of bucks for the smaller ones to well over $50 for the more complex models. He had his sights set on a Bumblebee Camaro Transformer that cost $27.99. Now, in our household, poker chips were valued at $0.25 each, so he quickly realized that getting his hands on Bumblebee was going to take some serious saving.

Meanwhile, the Dollar Store was full of off-brand transforming toys that he could easily afford with a few days worth of chip earning. The dilemma was real—should he blow his chips on the cheap knock-off and have something now, or should he hold out and save up for the real deal? To his credit, he opted to wait, learning a valuable lesson in patience and delayed gratification along the way. The day he finally had enough chips to buy that Bumblebee Transformer was a victory like no other.

Now, think about it from an adult perspective. How often do we face the same type of decision? Do you spend your hard-earned money on a quick fix or save up for something you really want? When children are asked to pay for something themselves, their perspective shifts. Suddenly, they're a lot more discerning about where those chips go.

In using the chip system, not only are you teaching your child about the value of money and the benefits of saving, but you're also creating a family dynamic where everyone's contributing to the "family pot" of good behavior and positive outcomes. It's a win-win—just like a successful hand in poker. So, next time your child is eyeing that shiny new toy, hand them a chip or two, and watch as they learn to play the long game, one chip at a time.

## ENHANCING THE BEHAVIOR MODIFICATION PLAN: ESTABLISHING A PAY PERIOD

So, you've got your poker chip behavior modification plan up and running, and things are going smoothly. But let's up the ante a bit, shall we? Enter the concept of the "pay period," a clever addition that mirrors how we adults get paid—weekly, bi-monthly, or monthly. The idea here is simple: designate a specific time when your child can exchange their hard-earned chips for cold, hard cash.

One of the perks of having a weekly pay period is that it builds a bit of suspense and encourages saving. If your child cashes out all their chips as soon as they earn them, they might be left high and dry with nothing to lose as a consequence for bad behavior. So, just like that escrow account your mortgage lender loves so much, it's a good idea to set a rule that keeps a minimum balance in their chip bank. This way, there's always something at stake, and the system keeps its teeth.

One of the great things about the chip system is that it gives children some skin in the game. They get to decide how to spend their chips—whether to blow them on a quick reward or save up for something big. Waiting a week or more between cash-outs gets them closer to those long-term savings goals, teaching them patience and the value of delayed gratification. Many of us take pride in our paychecks and think twice before splurging on something frivolous because we know how much work went into earning that money. The hope is that our children will develop that same sense of pride, becoming more mindful about how they spend their chips.

And let's not forget the power dynamics here. As parents, we're the ones holding the purse strings. Sometimes it's easy to forget that *we're in control*, and we inadvertently hand that control over to our children. But by managing the chip system effectively, we can maintain that balance of authority while teaching our children valuable lessons in responsibility, financial management, and the idea that effort equals reward.

REFLECTION QUESTIONS:

- Do you think a "payment-style" behavioral modification plan—like rewards for good behavior—would work for your children? Why or why not? Would it motivate them, or turn every chore into a negotiation?

- As a parent, when do you feel like you've lost control of a situation—whether it's a bedtime battle or a public meltdown?

- What strategies help you regain control without feeling like you're running a tiny, chaotic kingdom?

- How do you strike a balance between rewarding good behavior and fostering intrinsic motivation (you know, the dream where they clean their room *just because*)?

THE SLIPPERY SLOPE OF MOTIVATION AND CONSEQUENCES

In the chip-based behavior modification system, children can not only earn chips for good behavior, completing tasks, or reaching specific goals, but they can also lose chips for misbehavior or failing to meet expectations (setting the house on fire has consequences!). Just as quickly as they can accumulate chips, they can see them disappear if they choose to act out or disregard the rules. This dynamic mirrors real-life consequences where positive actions are rewarded, and negative behaviors have tangible costs. The possibility of losing chips adds a layer of accountability, teaching children that their actions have immediate and direct consequences, both positive and negative. By incorporating the potential for loss, the chip system helps reinforce the importance of making good choices and understanding that privileges and rewards must be earned and can also be forfeited.

This is where the beauty of poker chips comes in. They're not real money, but they hold value in your household economy. Taking away a chip as a consequence is much easier—and less emotionally charged—than trying to yank back a $10 bill you already handed over. And if that money's already been spent? Good luck. But a chip? That's just a token, and it's easier for your child to part with, especially if they know there's a way to earn it back.

I'll never forget the time my daughter, who was four at the time, had an epic meltdown when my husband picked her up from daycare. She was playing outside, and when he told her he'd already packed up her things, she completely lost it. She threw a toy at him, called him "stupid" in the parking lot, and announced that she wanted to move to the jungle. Later, we found out she was just upset because she wanted to show off a toy she'd earned at preschool before it got packed away. In response, we took away her tablet for three days—a pretty big deal for her at the time. On the first day, she understood why she couldn't use her tablet, but by the second and third days, the connection between her meltdown and the punishment had faded. We had to keep reminding her why she didn't have her tablet, which only made her more upset with us. That's when we realized that for a four-year-old, immediate consequences were way more effective.

As children get older, they can handle delayed consequences

better, but younger children really benefit from quick feedback. It's kind of like when you overspend during Christmas shopping, using a credit card for all those gifts. The consequences of your overspending don't hit until the bill arrives later, and by then, the thrill of shopping has faded, making it harder to connect the dots between your actions and the resulting high credit card bill. Without that connection, it's tough to change your behavior.

REFLECTION QUESTIONS:

- Can you think of a time when a consequence you gave your child didn't have the intended effect because too much time had passed since the behavior? How did your child respond, and what did you take away from the experience?

- Has that situation changed how you apply consequences now? Do you try to address behavior more quickly to create a stronger connection between actions and outcomes?

- On the flip side, have you ever faced a consequence in your own life that didn't come soon enough to influence your behavior? How did the delay affect your motivation to change?

- What lessons from your own experiences with consequences help shape how you guide your child's understanding of accountability today?

My hope is that our children will start to see their growing stash of chips as a badge of honor, proof of their good behavior and diligent chore-doing. As parents, it's our job to dish out praise alongside those chips, with the goal that the good behavior sticks around longer than the leftover Halloween candy.

When I first rolled out this behavior modification plan at home, I made sure their chip jars were front and center, where they could keep a close eye on their progress. But here's the catch: for this system to work, we parents have to be on our game too. That means being crystal clear about what actions earn chips and what antics will cause those chips to vanish like magic.

Take, for example, the time my five-year-old son asked for a chip as a reward for eating his supper. My husband and I had to think this one through—was scarfing down spaghetti really worthy of a chip? We decided that eating supper was just part of the daily grind, so no chips would be handed out for that. We figured if dinner time ever turned into a battle of wills, we might revisit the idea, but for now, no chips for simply showing up to the dinner table or brushing teeth. These are baseline expectations in our household. But hey, the beauty of this system is that it's as flexible as a yoga instructor, so if we need to tweak it to keep the peace, we can.

When our son hit first grade, his school had this cool system where children could "clip up" or "clip down" on a color chart based on their behavior. Everyone started on green, and depending on their actions, they could move up to bright and shiny colors or down to gloomier shades. We thought, why not bring this idea home? So, we started giving our son a chip every time he clipped up at school and taking one away when he clipped down. It was a way to keep the school's expectations in sync with our own at home, kind of like a double reinforcement plan.

The secret sauce to making any behavior modification system work is consistency. As long as we, the parents, stay firm on what earns chips and what loses them, the system has a real shot at encouraging good behavior in our children—plus, it's a great way to keep them motivated and maybe even a little bit competitive.

# CHAPTER 12

## LEARNED HELPLESSNESS

Poker is a complex game that requires practice and skill—two things I've never quite mastered. Sure, I know the rules, but I wouldn't exactly call myself a poker pro. It probably doesn't help that whenever I play with my family, my brother, who airs a bit on the side of believing he knows everything, is always there to tell me what to do. If he's out of a hand, he'll peek at my cards and whisper, "You should raise," or "Fold now while you still can." While I appreciate his help, it's not doing me any favors in the long run. Instead of learning the game myself, it made me reliant on him to make decisions for me.

This scenario isn't too different from the classic parental mantra: "It's just easier if I do it myself." I've lost count of how many times I've said this. But what we often overlook is that by doing things for our children that they're perfectly capable of doing themselves, we're not really making things easier. In fact, we're making it harder—harder for them to learn, harder for them to become independent, and harder for us to break the cycle of dependence.

Let's take the morning ritual of getting the children dressed. It used to be a daily battle. My children would dawdle, put their arms through the wrong holes, or take forever to pick an outfit. Meanwhile, I'd be in full-on panic mode, thinking, "We're going to be late! How can it take this long to put on pants?" The temptation to just step in and do it for them was strong, especially when I knew I could do it faster and better. Sound familiar? But every time I dressed them myself, I was sending the message that they couldn't handle it on their own. I was setting them up to expect that someone would always swoop in and save the day.

That's when I had to ask myself, "Am I enabling my children's dependence on me just to ease my own anxiety?" Whether it was the fear of being late or the worry that they wouldn't dress themselves "properly," the result was the same: I was stunting their growth. To reference the earlier example, my brother didn't want to see me make a poker move he wouldn't make. Similarly, I didn't want to see my children make choices that didn't align with my own standards—whether in their outfits or their time management. But just as I'll never become a confident poker player if I keep leaning on my brother, my children won't learn to be self-sufficient if I keep stepping in to do things for them.

The lesson here is clear: If we want our children to develop confidence and independence, we have to give them the space to make their own decisions—even if those decisions aren't the ones we would make. It's about letting go of our own anxieties and trusting that, with practice, they'll learn to navigate life's challenges on their own. After all, how can they ever get good at playing the game if we're always holding their cards?

When I was 14 and sporting a mouthful of braces, monthly check-up appointments with the dentist had to be scheduled as a part of their routine maintenance. I incorrectly assumed my mother would take care of the appointment scheduling—because why wouldn't she right? Wrong. When I asked her to make the appointment, her response was, "They aren't my braces, so why would I make the appointment?" I was both annoyed and a little anxious about making the call myself. I had hoped she would take care of it, so

I could continue living in blissful ignorance of the adult world of scheduling and responsibility.

But here's the thing about anxiety: if you don't challenge it, it doesn't just quietly disappear—it festers. Although that first phone call was nerve-wracking, I made it. I confronted my anxiety and resisted the urge to let my mother handle it. If she had made the appointment for me, I would have gladly let her, missing out on an important life lesson. Looking back, I realize how valuable that lesson was: stepping out of your comfort zone and challenging your anxiety can transform something daunting into something routine. Eventually, calling the dentist became so normal that it no longer bothered me—it became my new norm.

Fast forward to my time as a collegiate advisor and therapist, where I observed a wide range of parental involvement. Some parents were like my brother during poker games—unwilling to let go, always stepping in to "help" their students manage everything from class schedules to laundry. It seemed these students hadn't been given the chance to fail—a concept that, on the surface, sounds counterintuitive. Who would want their child to fail? Yet, as much as I struggle with this as a parent, I've come to realize that shielding children from anxiety and failure can be just as harmful as ignoring their struggles altogether. When we eliminate anxiety or failure from their lives, we deny them the opportunity to develop the coping skills they'll need when challenges inevitably arise.

I remember working with a college student who was also an athlete, competing in Track & Field. We compared his ability to cope with anxiety to his ability to perform in his sport. Just as an athlete needs to stretch, run, and practice daily to improve, our children need to practice their coping skills to handle life's stresses. If an athlete skips training, their performance will suffer. Similarly, if we don't allow our children to face and manage their anxieties, they won't develop the resilience needed to navigate difficult situations.

During my time as an academic advisor, I often encountered parents who insisted that their child's academic schedule was too challenging and that they needed to be placed in easier classes. They were so concerned about their child failing that they were willing to risk delaying their graduation by overlooking the importance of course sequencing and prerequisites. This mindset is problematic because it prioritizes immediate comfort over long-term success. It's as if the parents would rather see their child in easier classes, avoiding the anxiety that comes with a challenge, rather than allowing them to grow through it.

As a parent myself, I grapple with the concept of "enabled anxiety" daily. Am I going to be the helicopter parent who shields my child from failure at all costs? It's difficult to watch your child struggle or experience anxiety, but preventing them from facing these challenges ultimately does them a disservice. A child who never learns to cope with anxiety may grow into an adult who struggles to function effectively. Trust me, that's not what any of us want for our children.

I remember a moment when my youngest son was four years old and asked me to peel an orange for him. Without even thinking, I took the orange and started peeling it. Then it hit me—I was doing exactly what I've been trying to teach others not to do. I was enabling my child to depend on me for something he could do himself. Sure, it would cause him some anxiety to peel the orange on his own, and he'd have to deal with the leftover strings and the mess, but it was crucial for him to experience that sense of independence. He needed to know that he could complete the task, even if it wasn't perfect. Admittedly, it was hard for me too; I didn't like seeing the juice splatter all over the new shirt I just bought him, or the somewhat mashed final product on the floor I had just cleaned. But what mattered most was that he felt the accomplishment of doing it by himself. It was a win for both of us.

When my oldest son was six, we signed him up for a wrestling program. He loved the practices, and I could see him starting to feel like a mini Olympic champion. But then came his first real wrestling meet. It was clear from the look on his face during that first match that this was nothing like the controlled, fun environment of practice. This was real competition, and it was tough for both of us. He lost by a single point and left the mat in tears. What he didn't realize was that there was another match waiting for him, and he was absolutely not on board with that.

Everything in me wanted to scoop him up and take him home. I wanted to tell him it was okay to quit and that he'd done enough. But I knew that if I let him give in to his fear and anxiety, I'd be teaching him that it's okay to give up when things get tough. So, despite his tearful pleas, I made him go back out there. He was pinned quickly, and when it was all over, he was mad at me—really mad. And I got it. But even though he didn't win a single contest, my husband and I couldn't have been prouder. He faced his fears, stepped back on that mat, and gave it another shot.

These experiences have shown me that allowing our children to face challenges and feel anxiety is *essential* for their growth. It's not easy to watch them struggle, but it's necessary. By doing so, we help them develop the resilience they'll need to navigate life's inevitable difficulties.

REFLECTION QUESTIONS:

- When have you found yourself thinking, *"It's just easier if I do it myself"*? Was it about saving time, avoiding a mess, or sidestepping a potential meltdown?

- Have you noticed any long-term consequences of enabling your child in these moments—like increased dependence or missed opportunities for them to learn?

- How does your child's anxiety (or frustration) influence your decision-making as a parent? Do you ever choose the path of least resistance just to keep the peace?

- While it's tempting to just peel the orange yourself, how can you remind yourself that sometimes, letting them struggle a little leads to sweeter victories—for both of you?

## HOMEWORK AND EXERCISES

- **Reflect on Your "It's Easier If I Do It" Moments:** Take a few minutes to think about those times when you've stepped in to do something for your child that they could have done themselves. Was it easier for you in the short term? Sure, maybe—less mess, fewer tears, and less time. But consider the long-term impact this might have on your child's independence and confidence. Write down at least three examples where you swooped in to save the day, and then reflect on how this could be affecting your child's growth. And hey, don't feel too guilty; we've all been there.

- **Identify Opportunities for Independence:** Over the next week, start playing a little game I like to call, "Spot the Independence Opportunity." Look for situations where you can encourage your child to take on tasks they might usually rely on you for—like making their bed, preparing their own snack, or even scheduling their own appointments if they're old enough. Start small and gradually increase the level of responsibility as they build confidence.

- **Challenge Your Own Anxiety:** Let's be real: sometimes the hardest part of letting our children do things on their own is dealing with our own anxiety. Do you find yourself stepping in because you're worried about the outcome? What if they mess up? What if their head gets trapped in their shirt's left arm sleeve? This week, practice stepping back and letting your child navigate their own challenges. Keep a journal of your feelings during these moments—was it hard to watch? Did you bite your tongue? How did your child respond? Remember, you're building their resilience and yours!

- **Create a "Growth Opportunity" Plan:** We all have those areas where our children struggle or feel anxious, whether it's making phone calls, participating in sports, or completing a challenging task. Identify one area where your child could use a little push, and develop a plan to gradually increase their exposure to this activity. The goal is to support them, but not take over. You're their coach, not their personal assistant. Reflect on their progress and your own reactions as they gain confidence. It's a win-win situation—you get to relax a bit, and they get to grow.

- **Celebrate Small Wins:** Let's not forget to celebrate the victories! Each time your child successfully completes a task on their own, no matter how small, take a moment to acknowledge it. This positive reinforcement will help them associate independence with a sense of accomplishment. Keep a little "Victory Log" and write down these wins. Not only will this boost your child's confidence, but it will also remind you of how far they've come—and how your letting go is helping them grow.

- **Discuss and Debrief:** After your child has faced a challenge or tackled something on their own, take some time to sit down and chat about their experience. Ask them how they felt, what they found difficult, and what they learned. This debriefing not only reinforces the lesson but also opens up a line of communication that can help them process their emotions and build resilience. Plus, it's a great way to show them that you're proud of their efforts, even if things didn't go perfectly.

By engaging in these exercises, you'll not only help your child develop independence and coping skills, but you'll also gain insight into your own role in fostering their growth. Remember, the goal isn't to eliminate anxiety or challenges from your child's life—because let's face it, that's impossible—but to equip them with the tools they need to handle whatever comes their way. So, grab that metaphorical coach's whistle, and get ready to cheer them on from the sidelines!

# CHAPTER 13

## ALL-POWERFUL CHILDREN

In poker, the ultimate goal is to eliminate all other players, amassing all the chips to become the winner—the most powerful player at the table. This dynamic can be seen in our interactions with our children, where power struggles often arise. Are our children trying to eliminate us from their decision-making process? Maybe not literally, but figuratively, they are pushing back against anything that challenges their sense of control.

I had one of those parental "aha" moments when I realized I had inadvertently given my child too much power. It was a Sunday morning, and my husband and I were discussing our plans for the day. The day before, we had taken the children to the park, and on Sunday, we really wanted to spend some time on our canoe—a pastime that our then 4-year-old son didn't particularly enjoy. He found it "so boring." As we sat around, my husband asked our son if he'd like to go for a ride on the canoe, to which our son promptly responded, "No." Initially, we were ready to abandon our plans based on his response. That's when I had my realization—were we seriously letting our 4-year-old dictate our plans for the day? Apparently, we were, and that's precisely where we started losing our parental authority.

To my husband's surprise, I decided to take a different approach. I told our son, "You know what? I'm not asking you anymore; I'm telling you. We are going out on the canoe, and even if it's not your favorite thing, that's what we're doing." I sat him down and explained that, honestly, I hadn't wanted to go to the park the day before. It was hot, and I'm not exactly a fan of the park—But I made the decision to take him and his sister because I knew they enjoyed it. Sometimes, we do things we don't "feel like doing" because it makes the people we love happy (cue the sad Pixar music). I reminded him that his dad and I enjoy canoeing, and sometimes he has to do things he doesn't want to do for the sake of others—just like I did with the park. So, he might as well grab a paddle and start pretending to have fun!

Teaching empathy to a 4-year-old is just as easy as it sounds—so, basically, not at all. But it's essential. While my son didn't exactly jump for joy at the idea of doing something he didn't want to do, it was important for him to understand that being considerate of others' feelings is a crucial part of life. If children never experience a little powerlessness or anxiety, they'll be in for a shock when real life throws them a curveball. As parents, we're walking a tightrope—trying not to eliminate all anxiety from their lives, but also not dumping a bucket of it on their heads. It's a balancing act. Teaching them that sometimes they've got to step outside their comfort zone for the sake of others is a life lesson that'll serve them well.

In that moment, I realized that parenting is as much about guiding our children through their emotions as it is about setting boundaries. It's about showing them that life involves compromise, consideration, and sometimes doing things we don't want to do. By standing firm and making decisions that balance the needs of everyone in the family, we help our children understand that they are part of a larger community, where everyone's feelings and preferences matter—not just their own.

REFLECTION QUESTIONS:

- Do your children sometimes end up dictating your plans —whether it's what's for dinner, weekend activities, or the sacred TV remote. How often do you find yourself adjusting to meet their preferences?

- How do they react when things don't go their way? Are they flexible, frustrated, or full-on meltdown mode?

- When your child struggles with anxiety or disappointment over not getting what they want, how do you help them cope? What strategies have worked to ease their frustration while still setting healthy boundaries?

- How do you balance being empathetic with maintaining structure—without feeling like you're constantly negotiating with a tiny, emotionally volatile CEO?

Take a moment to grab your favorite beverage (trust me, you'll need it) and get ready to do some parenting. We're about to dig deep into those subtle (or not-so-subtle) power struggles that seem to pop up when your child decides they should be the one calling the shots:

- **Consider the Past:** Think back to those moments when your child took charge of your family's plans or flat-out refused to do something they didn't want to do. Take notes on how they react when they don't get their way— do they pout like a disgruntled cat or negotiate like their freedom depended on it? And how do you handle their anxiety?

- **Plan for the Next Power Struggle:** Identify an upcoming situation where a power struggle is likely and strategize how you'll assert your parental authority while still acknowledging their feelings (because we're not monsters, after all).

- **Journal the Outcome:** After the event, take some time to journal about what went down. What worked? What didn't? How many bribes, if any, were involved in restoring peace?

- **Balance Empathy with Boundaries:** By reflecting on these experiences, learn how to balance empathy with firm boundaries, helping your child understand that they're part of a larger community where everyone's needs matter—not just theirs.

After completing these exercises, take a moment to appreciate the effort you've put in. Balancing empathy with authority isn't easy, but it's a crucial part of raising children who understand that they're part of a team—and not always the team captain. So, treat yourself to something nice (you've earned it), and get ready to tackle the next parenting challenge with newfound confidence!

# CHAPTER 14

## PASSIVE/AGGRESSIVE PLAYERS

In poker, while everyone plays by the same basic rules, each player's strategy can differ wildly, making it a challenging game to teach and learn. Each player's approach influences the decisions they make throughout the game, and much like in parenting, strategy is often shaped by past experiences and individual personality. If we're honest, what demands more strategic planning than parenting?

It's a high-stakes game where you're betting with your legacy, and your sanity. As such, poker players can either lean toward being more passive in their style of play or more aggressive in their style of play.

Similarly, parents can fall somewhere on the spectrum between passive and aggressive. When I think about these two types of parents, I consider how and when they choose to intervene in their child's life. A passive parent might let situations "play out," like a poker player waiting for the right moment to raise. They believe in the value of letting children navigate challenges on their own—basically, they're betting on their child's ability to figure it out. An aggressive parent, however, might step in more quickly, like a player who goes all in at the slightest hint of a good hand. They take a hands-on approach to guide or protect their child, sometimes with the intensity of a linebacker charging downfield.

I remember a moment that perfectly illustrated these different parenting styles. I had taken my two children to the city park to meet up with a friend who had a 4-year-old and an infant. As our children played on the equipment, a slightly older boy sauntered over from some picnic tables in the distance. He zeroed in on my daughter, who was much smaller than him, and started getting in her face, putting his hands on her shoulders, and shaking her slightly while making weird faces. It wasn't violent, but it was enough to make my "mama bear" instincts twitch. Instead of swooping in immediately, I decided to channel my inner passive parent and see how things played out—probably because I hadn't had my coffee yet and was curious if my daughter would handle it like a pro or just scream for backup.

The boy soon turned his attention to my son, who was both intrigued and frustrated by the boy's rough play. My son, hesitantly but curiously, followed him to a nearby water fountain, where the boy promptly sprayed him with water. Great—now we had impromptu water sports in the park. I wasn't thrilled about it, but what really irked me was that the boy's parents were lounging far away in the shelter, blissfully unaware of the chaos their child was stirring up. This was passive parenting taken to the extreme, where their son was practically auditioning for "Most Annoying Child at the Park," and they were missing the whole show.

As much as I wanted to march over and hand them a "Parent of the Year" award (with a heavy dose of sarcasm), I couldn't help but feel a bit sorry for the boy. He was clearly starved for attention, desperately seeking it by messing with other children. No one was pushing him on the swing or cheering him on as he went down the slide—he was a one-man wrecking crew, with no audience.

Not all passive parents are like these oblivious ones. Some are fully aware of what's happening but choose to let situations unfold naturally, believing it helps their children develop coping skills and problem-solving abilities without constant parental intervention.

This approach can indeed foster resilience and independence, but like all strategies, it requires careful consideration of when to step in and when to step back. Each approach has its place. The key is knowing when to apply it. Whether we're talking about poker or parenting, it's clear that the most successful players—or parents—are those who can adapt their strategy to the situation at hand.

REFLECTION QUESTIONS:

- How would you describe your parenting style—are you more passive, letting things play out naturally, or assertive, stepping in to take charge when needed?

- How do your children handle conflicts? Do you notice any differences compared to how you managed conflicts when you were their age?

- What do those differences say about your parenting style versus the way your parents raised you?

- Have you intentionally tried to shift certain patterns from your own upbringing, or do you find yourself repeating some of the same approaches (for better or worse)?

When I look back on my own experiences, the differences between how I parent and how my parents did are pretty stark. My folks were more of the "let them figure it out" type, while my husband and I tend to lean into a more assertive style. I mean, if there's a referee needed for a sibling squabble, that's usually me with the whistle. This balancing act is so situational, too. Sometimes stepping in is the right call, and other times, it's better to let things play out.

I've had similar dilemmas when I was a college mental health therapist. It was a constant juggling act to figure out how much to intervene with each student. They were technically adults, but they were also navigating the choppy waters of life away from home for the first time. Some needed a gentle nudge, while others needed a full-on lifeline. The trick was figuring out which approach worked best for each individual.

REFLECTION QUESTIONS:

- Have you ever found yourself in a situation where you didn't want to enable someone's behavior, but also didn't want to abandon them? What made the situation so difficult to navigate?

- How did you strike a balance between offering support and setting healthy boundaries?

- Looking back, do you feel you handled it effectively, or are there things you would approach differently now?

- What lessons did you take from that experience, and how has it influenced your approach to supporting others— whether it's with your children, friends, or family?

EXERCISES

- **Reflect on Your Parenting Style:** Spend some time thinking about whether you tend to be more of a passive or aggressive parent. Are you the type to let things play out, or do you step in at the first sign of trouble? Write down a few examples from recent situations where you found yourself either stepping back or stepping in. How did those situations turn out? Did your approach work, or did it backfire?

- **Compare Your Parenting to Your Parents:** Think about how your parents handled conflicts or challenges when you were a child. Were they more passive or aggressive in their approach? Now, compare that to how you handle similar situations with your own children. Write a brief reflection on the differences and similarities. How has your upbringing influenced your current parenting style?

- **Identify a Situation to Apply a Different Strategy:** Pick an upcoming scenario where you'd normally do your parenting thing—whether it's going full drill sergeant or channeling your inner Zen monk. Now, here's the fun part: do the exact opposite. If you're usually hands-on, try stepping back and letting the chaos unfold. If you're more of a "let it ride" type, dive in and take charge like you're auditioning for the role of "Boss Parent 2025." Afterward, take a moment to reflect on how it went—did your new approach lead to peace, harmony, and a small parade in your honor? Or did it just reinforce why you usually do things your way? Either way, it's all in the name of experimentation...and hopefully, an education.

- **Journal Your Playground Experiences:** Reflect on how you handled conflicts as a child compared to how your children handle them now. What are the key differences? Consider how societal changes, parenting trends, or personal experiences might have influenced these differences. Write down your thoughts and how they relate to your current parenting decisions.

- **Discuss with a Partner or Friend:** Have a conversation with your partner, a friend, or another parent about how they handle the balance between being passive and aggressive in their parenting. Share your own experiences and ask for their perspective. This exercise can help you gain new insights and perhaps even some fresh strategies to try out in your own parenting journey.

By completing these exercises, you'll get a better grip on your parenting style, how it stacks up against others, and how to tweak your approach for different situations. Remember, there's no magic formula in parenting—just like in poker, it's all about reading the situation.

# CHAPTER 15

## #SORRYNOTSORRY

Poker is a ruthless game, one where there's only one winner—the person who holds all the chips at the end. This cutthroat competition is precisely what draws people to the game. There's no room for apologies when you take someone out; in fact, that's the whole point.

In our daily interactions, especially with our children, apologies are far more common. The frequency with which we apologize—or don't—can have a profound impact on our relationships, not just with our children but with others as well. Apologizing is essentially an admission of wrongdoing, a way of saying, "I made a mistake, and I'm willing to own up to it." This act of taking responsibility puts us in a vulnerable position.

You've probably heard some parents apologizing for everything under the sun: "I'm sorry I didn't get you that toy," "I'm sorry your peanut butter and jelly was cut in triangles not in rectangles ." And sure, sometimes an apology is the right call, like when you accidentally step on your child's favorite LEGO creation (which, let's be honest, probably hurt you more than them). Excessive apologizing will inadvertently increase your vulnerability and diminish your power in the relationship. The more vulnerable a parent becomes, the less power they hold, and the more power the child gains.

It's not about banning apologies, but about using them wisely. If your children start expecting you to apologize for everything, even things that aren't your fault, they might start thinking they're always right. And let's face it, they're not always right—like that time they swore they could jump off the couch and land like a ninja (spoiler: they couldn't).

Take this example: I previously mentioned my son's obsession with his Bumblebee Transformer. One day, he accidentally snapped off a tiny piece and immediately wanted my husband to drop everything and fix it. This happened when my husband and I had just gotten home from work. We were juggling various tasks—feeding our then 8-month-old baby, preparing dinner, sorting out homework, and addressing all the other responsibilities that demanded our attention. So my husband said, "I'm sorry, I can't fix it right now." Now, what was he apologizing for? By apologizing, my husband might have unintentionally suggested that he was in the wrong for not fixing the toy right away, which wasn't the case.

A more appropriate response might have been, "I understand that having your Bumblebee Transformer fixed right away is important to you, but I have other priorities at the moment. It's important to me too, so I'll fix it for you after dinner and once the baby is asleep."

On the flip side, never apologizing can indicate that a parent is unwilling to take responsibility for their actions, perhaps seeking to maintain a disproportionate level of power in the relationship. The idea of being vulnerable to someone else can be incredibly difficult, especially if it feels like that vulnerability might lead to some kind of risk. Some parents might go to great lengths to avoid taking the blame for something, even when they are clearly at fault.

So, here's the deal: Apologize when it's necessary, but don't hand out sorry's like they're going out of style. Keep the power dynamic in check, and recognize that being overly apologetic can shift the dynamics of power in a relationship in ways that may not be beneficial.

REFLECTION QUESTIONS:

- Can you think of someone in your life who either over-apologizes or never seems to apologize at all? What do you think drives that behavior—vulnerability, pride, or something else entirely?

- How do power dynamics play into their behavior? Is there a pattern where the person with less control tends to say "sorry" more often, while the one calling the shots rarely does?

- How do these patterns affect your interactions with them? Have you ever found yourself adjusting your own behavior in response to their apology habits?

- What lessons can you take from observing these dynamics, and how might they influence the way you handle apologies in your own relationships?

# CHAPTER 16

## YOU ARE NOT THEIR FRIEND

As I mentioned earlier, poker is a ruthless game where there's only one winner. In the heat of the game, couples stop being couples, and friends stop being friends; every player is out for themselves. It's an "every person for themselves" mentality.

I remember a story about my parents in a poker tournament at the Golden Nugget in Las Vegas. They both made it to the final table, and eventually, it came down to just the two of them—heads up, the last players standing. The dealer, noticing they were married, assumed they would "chop" the pot, meaning they'd split the winnings evenly. But my parents? Oh, they were not like other couples. For them, it was either his pot or hers. There was no "chop chop the pot" for them. They played it out, and to my mother's dismay, my father came out on top. Let's just say, the ride home was a bit frosty.

I use this example because poker isn't about "going easy" on someone else—it's about winning. It's about knowing your end goal and doing everything in your power to achieve it. And yes, this same ruthless mentality can apply to parenting.

Here's the deal: you are NOT their friend. Friends aren't, or shouldn't be, responsible for raising you. As a parent, your role is to win—where winning means being a good role model and instilling the importance of good behavior. You can love your children fiercely, believe they are the most amazing beings ever born, but that doesn't exempt you from the responsibility of parenting them properly. Like poker, parenting can be harsh, and yes, sometimes you've got to play the tough hand.

Just as there's an inevitability in poker that you'll upset other players by eliminating them, there's a certainty that you'll upset your children with your parenting decisions. But that should never deter you from doing what needs to be done to raise them well. You can tell them that they can't eat cookies for dinner—and you know it's going to cause a meltdown, but you also know that carrots are better for them in the long run (even though they might "hate you" for it).

This ruthlessness also extends to defending and protecting your child. Just as poker players defend their chip stack and reputation, parents instinctively want to protect their children and ensure their safety. I recall a situation where our daughter was playing outside right after a snowstorm. She was collecting large icicles when a neighborhood child asked to hold one. When she handed it to him, he broke it in half and laughed. She came inside crying, deeply upset by what had happened. I was furious that another child had intentionally hurt her feelings. It took all my willpower not to march over and give that child a piece of my mind.

This protective instinct is as fierce as a poker player's drive to win, and it's a crucial part of parenting. Just as in poker, where players defend their position, parents must be ready to defend and protect their children, ensuring they feel safe, loved, and secure— even if it means going into Mama Bear mode and unleashing the wrath of a thousand cubs.

So while I'm not their friend, I need them to know that I'm *always* in their corner, fiercely defending and protecting them from harm. That's my job as a parent, and it's one I take seriously. Sure, there will be times when I have to be stern, cancel their fun because I'm worried about their well-being, or play the role of the big bad wolf who appears more like an enemy than a bestie. But in those moments, it's important they understand that my role is to guard them like a hawk—whether it's from physical danger, emotional hurt, or anything else that might threaten their safety.

Being a parent isn't just about enforcing rules or setting boundaries; it's about making sure they thrive and grow into well-functioning adults who won't spend all their savings on impulse buys and snack food. Yes, sometimes that means saying no to fixing toys, bossing them around, or insisting they eat their vegetables for dinner. It might mean making tough decisions that they don't like, but those decisions are made out of love and a deep commitment to their well-being.

They might not always see it, but every time I say no or enforce a rule, it's because I'm thinking about their future. I'm thinking about the person they're becoming and the lessons they need to learn to navigate the world without getting lost. I may not always give them what they want, but they can always count on me to be there when it matters most. I will fight for them, stand up for them, and do everything in my power to keep them safe.

So, the next time you have to lay down the law and they push back, questioning why you can't just be their friend, take a moment to explain. Let them know that being their friend might seem like a blast, but being their parent is what's going to keep them safe, healthy, and on the right path. Friendship might be fun, but parenting is what truly makes a difference in their lives—and honestly, who else is going to make sure they eat their vegetables?

EXERCISES

- **Reflect on Your Parenting Decisions:** Think about a recent situation where you had to be the "bad guy" by enforcing a rule or saying no to something your child wanted. Write down what happened and how you felt afterward. Did you feel guilty? Proud? Relieved? Reflecting on these emotions can help you understand your own parenting style and reinforce why these tough decisions are necessary.

- **Identify Areas Where You Need to Be More Firm:** Consider where you might be letting your child have too much control. Are there areas where you've been more of a friend than a parent? Make a list of situations where you can step in and assert your authority more clearly, and plan out how you'll approach these moments in the future.

- **Explain Your Role to Your Child:** The next time your child pushes back against a decision, take the opportunity to sit down and explain your role as their parent. Use age-appropriate language to help them understand that your job is to protect and guide them, even when it means making decisions they don't like.

- **Practice "Parenting Poker Face":** In poker, maintaining a poker face is key to not giving away your strategy. Try practicing your own version of a "parenting poker face" by staying calm and composed during conflicts, even when your child is upset. This will help reinforce that your decisions are firm and not open to negotiation based on their reactions.

- **Create a "Defender of the Realm" Exercise:** With your child, create a fun activity where they role-play as a defender of their own imaginary realm. Discuss what it means to protect and care for something valuable, like a kingdom or a treasure. Then, explain how you, as their parent, are the defender of their well-being and how sometimes that means making tough choices. This can help them see your role in a new, more relatable light. This exercise is made easier if they have something that depends on them for survival, like a fish, or a puppy.

- **Set Clear Expectations and Consequences:** Revisit the rules and expectations in your household. Are they clear to your child? Take the time to outline specific behaviors that are non-negotiable and the consequences that will follow if those rules are broken. This will help your child understand that your role is not just about enforcing rules but also about keeping them safe and teaching them important life skills.

- **Journal About a "Mama Bear" Moment:** Write about a time when you went into "Mama Bear" mode, fiercely protecting your child from harm or hurt. How did you handle the situation, and what was the outcome? Reflect on how this instinct to protect is a crucial part of your role as a parent, and how it sometimes means making unpopular decisions for the greater good.

By completing these exercises, you'll strengthen your ability to balance authority with empathy, ensuring that while you may not be your child's friend, you're always their greatest defender and guide.

# CHAPTER 17

## THE NEED TO BE UNIQUE

In the high-stakes world of professional poker, players are all about the same—highly skilled, razor-sharp, and ready to outplay their opponents. But here's the thing: they don't just want to be known for their poker face. Oh no, they want to stand out! It's a game within a game—who can wear the most outrageous hat, the quirkiest sunglasses, or carry around the weirdest good luck charm? It's their way of saying, "Yeah, I'm just as good as the rest of you, but I'm also totally my own person, so don't you forget it!"

As a parent, I've noticed that children are a lot like these poker pros—they've got this deep, burning desire to be unique, to stand out from the sibling pack, and to make sure that you, dear parent, see them as the special snowflakes they are. And honestly, who can blame them? Nobody wants to be lost in the shuffle—or worse, forgotten! So, they'll do what it takes to make sure they're on your radar.

Take my oldest son, for example. When he was about four or five, he had this thing where he'd constantly point out how different he was from his younger sister. "I'm your big boy, and she's just the baby," or "You call me a goofball, but not her." It was like he was waving a flag that said, "Notice me, notice how I'm not like her!"—as if I could ever mix them up! But to him, it was crucial to carve out his own little corner in my world, distinct from his sister's.

It's totally human to want to feel special, to have something that makes us stand out from the crowd. I mean, we all want to be Greg Raymer with the lizard-eye glasses or Phil Laak with the signature hoodie, right? The same goes for our children. They need to know that, in the poker game of life, they're not just another player at the table—they're the ones with the coolest accessory, the most unique nickname, the player everyone remembers.

When our youngest son was born, I realized that acknowledging each of my children's unique identities wasn't just a nice thing to do —it was essential. I have my oldest son, my youngest son, and my middle child, who also happens to be my only daughter. And believe me, I let them know that they each have a special role in our family. It's not about playing favorites (even if I did, I'd never admit it!), but about making sure they each feel that they have a spot in our family that's uniquely theirs.

By recognizing and celebrating these differences, I'm helping them see that they're not just another face in the crowd—they're each their own star. And trust me, in a house with multiple children, that's a big deal. I want them to know that they're not just loved, but loved for exactly who they are.

REFLECTION QUESTIONS:

- How do you highlight your children's unique qualities and help them embrace what makes them stand out? Are there specific moments when you've seen them shine as individuals?

- Do you notice your children trying to set themselves apart from siblings or peers? How do you support their need for individuality without creating unnecessary competition?

- On the flip side, have you observed any benefits to recognizing their similarities? How does shared common ground strengthen their bond—or your bond with them?

- In the game of parenting, what strategies have you found most effective in balancing their need for both uniqueness and connection?

# CHAPTER 18

## HIT ME

In the high-stakes world of poker, discipline is paramount, and the consequences for cheating or breaking the rules are severe. Professional poker games, especially those played in casinos or major tournaments, are governed by strict regulations to ensure fair play. If a player is caught cheating—whether through collusion, marking cards, or using hidden devices—they can expect swift and decisive action.

Immediate penalties may include the forfeiture of their chips, disqualification from the game, and permanent bans from the casino or tournament circuit. Beyond these immediate consequences, cheating can also demolish a player's reputation, making it nearly impossible for them to find a seat at any reputable poker table in the future. The poker community is small and gossipy—word of your misdeeds will spread faster than a viral cat video. In some cases, depending on the jurisdiction and the severity of the offense, legal action might also be pursued. Casinos are equipped with super high-tech surveillance systems, and tournament officials are trained to detect and prevent dishonest behavior, ensuring that the integrity of the game is upheld at all times. In high-stakes poker, the risks of cheating far outweigh any potential rewards. So the message is clear: break the rules, and the punishment will be severe!

As parents, one of our top priorities—right after making sure our children don't draw on the walls or flush toys down the toilet—is teaching them to take responsibility for their actions. We're aiming to raise future adults who don't point fingers at the dog when they forget to do their homework Most importantly, we aim to raise future adults who understand the rules of the game they're playing and are fully aware of the consequences of breaking those rules.

When it comes to disciplining children, parents have a wide array of tools at their disposal, each with its own set of philosophies and controversies. There's the classic *Time-Out*—a temporary banishment to the Thinking Chair, where children are supposed to reflect on their actions but most likely just plot their next move. Then there's *Positive Reinforcement*, which is basically bribing your children to behave with the promise of stickers, extra screen time, or, if you're really desperate, a pony. Some parents go the "Natural Consequences" route, letting children experience the reality of their choices—like when they refuse to wear a coat and then learn first-hand that winter is not, in fact, just a suggestion. Logical Consequences are similar but are more directly tied to the offense, like losing Wi-Fi privileges for ignoring homework. Grounding is another classic, where the social butterfly is clipped of its wings, sentenced to a weekend of quality time with its parents. Stern Talks, also known as the "Let Me Explain How the World Works" speech, aim to instill moral values but often result in eye-rolls and glazed-over stares. And then, there's Corporal Punishment, the most controversial tool in the kit.

This is a delicate and often controversial topic: *hitting* as a form of discipline, specifically hitting a child as a consequence for their actions. Yes, I'm talking about the age-old debate of whether or not to give a well-placed swat on the behind when your little angel behaves in ways that are a bit dark.

But before we dive in, let me throw out a big disclaimer: this is *our* personal approach, and I fully get that it might not align with how other parents roll. You do you, as they say, and we'll do us. I strongly believe that each family should do what works best for them and their children.

When each of our three children hit that magical age of two, they all seemed to adopt hitting as their go-to frustration management technique. It was like their tiny fists were saying, "I don't have the words yet, so here's a smack instead!" Take our daughter, for example. When my husband would pick her up from daycare, and she wasn't ready to leave because she was still knee-deep in whatever toddler shenanigans were going on, she'd let him know exactly how she felt—with a good ol' smack, while he was trying to carry her out of the building.

Now, I'm sure my husband had his own moments of frustration, probably picturing the headlines: "Dad Takes Punch From Pint-Sized Boxer" but he *never* hit her back. We're not exactly fans of the "fight fire with fire" approach, or in this case, the "fight hitting with hitting" strategy. Our goal was never to make her feel the sting of her own medicine or to scare her into never raising a hand again. What we really wanted was to teach her that there are way better ways to express her feelings—ones that don't involve turning into Mike Tyson every time she's upset.

For us, relying on fear—whether through the threat of a good old-fashioned spanking or some other form of physical punishment—felt like a temporary solution that might temporarily stop the behavior, but won't actually fix the problem. I'll be the first to admit that I was spanked as a child, and while it did strike fear into me when I got caught doing something wrong, it didn't exactly inspire me to become a model citizen. More often than not, it just made me scared and angry with my parents and better at not getting caught.

But here's the million-dollar question: did those spankings actually make me reflect on my behavior and realize I needed to change, or did they just fuel my inner rebel and make me resent my parents' chosen method of discipline? Even as a child, I remember the irony of getting spanked for hitting my sister. It's like, "Wait a minute—so hitting is wrong, but only when *I* do it?"

In our family, we decided that the "do as I say, not as I do" approach wasn't the approach we wanted to take. We wanted our children to learn from their mistakes, not just be scared of the inevitable spanking. The goal was to teach them to understand the impact of their actions and take responsibility for them—not just to live in fear of the parental wrath descending upon them. By focusing on teaching appropriate behavior rather than doling out physical punishment, we hoped to instill values that would stick with them longer than the sting of a spanking. We wanted them to make better choices because they understood why it was the right thing to do, not because they were terrified of getting caught with their hand in the cookie jar (again).

*Do you agree or disagree? Why or why not?*

## HOMEWORK AND EXERCISES:

- **Reflect on Your Discipline Strategies:** Take a week to observe your go-to discipline moves. Are you the "Time-Out Tyrant," or do you sprinkle positive reinforcement like confetti? Do you favor the "let-them-learn-the-hard-way" natural consequences, or are you all about the stern talking-to? Jot down which methods you lean on like a crutch and try to figure out why.

- **Try a New Approach:** If you're the kind of parent who's quick to slap on a time-out, why not mix things up? Maybe try logical consequences—like if they're caught red-handed breaking their sibling's toy, they have to let said sibling "borrow" their favorite toy for a while. Keep track of how this new approach goes: Did it inspire better behavior, or did your child come up with a new creative excuse that leaves you speechless?

- **Journal on Corporal Punishment:** Think back to your own childhood experiences with discipline, particularly if physical punishment was involved. Reflect on how it impacted you—did it teach you a lesson or just make you sneakier? How does that influence your views on spanking or other forms of corporal punishment today?

- **Discuss Discipline with Your Partner or a Fellow Parent:** Grab a coffee (or something stronger) and have a chat about the various discipline tools in your arsenal. Compare notes on what works and what just leads to eye-rolling. Do you find common ground, or do your views differ? How can you support each other in maintaining consistency?

- **Create a Family Discipline Plan:** Based on your reflections and discussions, draft a simple discipline plan for your household. Include the types of consequences you find most effective and the behaviors that warrant them. Keep it flexible enough to adapt to different situations, but clear enough that everyone knows the expectations and potential outcomes.

By working through these exercises, you'll gain a clearer understanding of how your discipline choices shape your child's behavior and development. Plus, you might just discover that a little reflection and adjustment can make the whole parenting game a bit less stressful and a lot more effective.

# CHAPTER 19

## THE KNOW-IT-ALL

In poker, there's nothing more infuriating than the "know-it-all" player. You know the type—the one who just can't resist offering unsolicited advice on every single hand. The problem? It messes with everyone else's game. When someone's constantly in your ear, it's hard to play your own hand, trust your own strategy, or even enjoy the game.

Now, let's flip the table. As a parent, it's easy to fall into the trap of being a "know-it-all" ourselves. We're the ones with life experience, after all. But just like in poker, being the all-knowing authority figure can backfire. While parents do hold authority because they are ultimately responsible for their child's well-being, this authority doesn't need to be enforced through sheer power. Ever catch yourself saying, "Because I said so!" when your child questions a decision? Sure, it's efficient, but it's also a conversation killer. It's the parenting equivalent of a bad bluff—an easy way out, but it doesn't win you the pot (or the respect). When a child feels that their thoughts and feelings are ignored, they may comply out of obligation rather than respect, which can hinder the development of a healthy, communicative relationship.

When was the last time you admired a boss or teacher for being distant, controlling, or rude? Yeah, probably never. The authority figures we respect are approachable, fair, and open to our input. So why not bring that same energy into our parenting? Ditch the "I'm the boss, and that's final" attitude, and start opening up the conversation.

Here's the magic trick: *negotiation.* Let's say your child is resisting bedtime—again. You could lay down the law and brace for a meltdown, or you could play it cool and offer a choice: "Do you want to go to bed now, or after one more book?" You're still the boss, but now your child feels like they have a say in the matter. It's a win-win.

When my oldest was a toddler, brushing teeth was a nightly battle. We're talking full-on tantrums, tears, the whole nine yards. My initial reaction? Threats of time-out, which only made things worse. Then I tried a new approach: "Do you want to brush your teeth before or after we read a book?" Boom! Instant cooperation. He still had to brush his teeth, but suddenly, he was in control of the situation—or at least, he felt like he was.

The beauty of offering choices is that it turns a potential power struggle into a partnership. Your child feels heard and respected, and you avoid unnecessary drama. Plus, you're teaching them valuable life skills—like negotiation, compromise, and decision-making—without them even realizing it. Sneaky, right?

Picture this: your child is standing in their underwear, refusing to get dressed. Instead of getting into a tug-of-war, you casually ask, "So, are you rocking the red shirt or the blue shirt today?" Suddenly, your child is weighing their options, feeling all grown up, and—voila!—they're dressed. You've just dodged a power struggle, and all it took was a little bit of choice magic.

It's important to strike a balance when offering choices. Providing too many options can overwhelm your child and may create a false sense of power, potentially leading to entitlement. If a parent continually asks, "Do you want carrots? Do you want peas? Do you want broccoli? Do you want spinach? What do you want? What will you eat?" it can lead the child to believe that the parent will cater to their every whim, ultimately undermining the negotiation process.

Choices are also fantastic for teaching children how to make decisions and handle the consequences. Making a good choice can enhance your child's confidence, while making a bad choice offers a learning opportunity. Let's say your child picks the blue shirt and then, halfway through the day, decides they hate it. Do you skip an important work meeting midday to change their shirt? Nope. You let them ride it out, and next time, they'll think a little harder about their decision.

For example, when it comes to behavioral choices, the stakes are higher. Let's say your child's having a major meltdown in the middle of the cereal aisle (because of course they are). Instead of issuing an ultimatum, you calmly offer a choice: "We can either finish shopping together, or we can leave the store and try again later. What's it gonna be?" They might not love the options, but they'll feel like they have a say—and often, that's enough to diffuse the situation.

Just as poker players must consider their options and make decisions that best suit their hand, providing options to your children allows them to feel more in control of their lives. This sense of control can be empowering and can contribute to their overall sense of security and well-being.

In our house, choices are a go-to strategy. My husband and I see it as a way to teach our children how to transition from bad behavior to good behavior without feeling like they're losing. By allowing our children to make decisions, we're helping them develop critical thinking skills, build resilience, and understand that their choices have consequences.

REFLECTION QUESTIONS:

- Have you noticed ways in which making decisions *for*

your child can become problematic? How does it affect their independence and confidence over time?

- How have you given your child the opportunity to make their own choices, even when you suspected it might not be the best decision? What did they learn from the outcome?

- How do you balance offering guidance without taking full control, allowing your child to experience both the rewards and consequences of their decisions?

- What strategies have helped you encourage better decision-making skills while still providing a safety net for learning moments?

# CHAPTER 20

## ENABLING

Lately, mental health diagnoses and suicidality have been on the rise, and while I can't pull specific numbers out of my hat, I have a strong hunch that a lack of coping skills plays a big role. Let's face it—if we're not exposed to anxiety, disappointment, or discomfort, how on earth are we supposed to learn how to deal with them? Think of it like this: if you always make your child's choices, you're basically training them to rely on you for everything, turning them into little decision-dependent creatures. This is what we call *enabling*—a well-meaning but ultimately unhelpful approach that keeps them from learning how to manage things on their own.

You know that phrase, "I've created a monster"? It usually means you've accidentally made your own life more complicated by enabling someone else. Sound familiar?

REFLECTION QUESTIONS:

- Can you think of a time when you unintentionally

enabled your child? What was the situation, and how did it affect their behavior moving forward?

- Do you know any adults who have been enabled throughout their lives? How would you describe their ability to handle responsibility, independence, or setbacks?

- How has observing those patterns in adults influenced your approach to parenting and setting boundaries?

- What steps can you take to ensure you're supporting your child's growth without enabling behaviors that might hold them back in the long run?

I mentioned this example earlier, but it's relevant here as well. Back when my older brother was out of a hand in poker, he'd coach me on when to fold, bid, or raise. (Side note: he's more aggressive, I'm more passive, so we'd often clash on strategy.) If I'd kept letting him call the shots, I'd never have learned to play the game myself. Sure, letting him decide would have spared me the sting of making a wrong choice, but I would've missed out on the chance to learn. There's real value in watching your child fail and learn from their mistakes.

I once read a blog post that really hit home. It was about two moms at a park. One mom was chilling on a bench while the other hovered near the playground. A child asked the bench mom for help climbing the stairs to the slide. She encouraged him to try on his own, but before he could, the other mom swooped in to help, which totally ticked off the bench mom. She wasn't being lazy—she was trying to teach her child to be independent and find out what he could do on his own.

Here's another example, this time from my own parenting journey. During my oldest son's first-grade parent-teacher conference, I got some surprising feedback. His friend mentioned that my son's locker was a disaster zone, and sure enough, his desk in the classroom was also a mess. To give you some context, I'm not a fan of clutter. My house isn't always spotless, but it's usually pretty tidy. It dawned on me that I'd been enabling my son's messiness by constantly picking up after him. Of course, he had a messy locker and desk—he hadn't learned to clean up after himself because I'd always done it for him. Talk about a wake-up call!

Enabling, no matter how well-intentioned, can stunt a child's growth in the long run. It keeps them from picking up crucial life skills like coping with disappointment, making decisions, and owning their actions. As parents, it's important to catch ourselves when we're enabling and consciously step back, giving our children the space to learn and grow through their own experiences. This not only sets them up for life's challenges but also helps them develop independence and resilience—key ingredients for future success.

REFLECTION QUESTIONS:

- Are there specific ways in which you find yourself enabling your child—whether it's doing tasks for them, avoiding conflict, or rescuing them from the consequences of their actions?

- Can you identify why you enable them? Is it driven by a desire to protect them, save time, reduce stress, or avoid emotional discomfort?

- How does this enabling behavior affect their independence and ability to learn from their mistakes?

- What small changes could you make to encourage responsibility while still offering support in a healthy, constructive way?

# CHAPTER 21

## CONSISTENCY IS KEY

My parents have a running joke about who's the more consistent poker player. They like to taunt and tease each other over who consistently racks up more points by the end of their poker session . In their local poker league, players earn points with each weekly win, and after an 8-week session, the top 24 point leaders duke it out in a tournament. Funny thing is, it's often the same faces in that final showdown, which tells you that *consistency really does pay off*. And guess what? Consistency is just as crucial in parenting as it is in poker—minus the chips and the bluffing, of course.

*"There are many ways in which parents can be consistent. How do you feel as though you provide consistency with your child/children?"*

We've all had that awkward encounter with an unpredictable adult. One minute they're snapping at you, the next they're all smiles! You never know what you're going to get, and that uncertainty can make you tread carefully around them. Now, imagine being a child and having to deal with that from a parent. One moment they're warm and fuzzy, and the next, they're cold and distant. That kind of inconsistency can make a child feel like they're walking on eggshells, never sure what version of mom or dad they're going to get.

I remember watching a dad playing with his two young daughters once. It started out as harmless roughhousing—he was on all fours, tossing the girls around playfully. They were giggling and trying to tackle him, though they were too tiny to do any real damage. But then, one of the girls accidentally kicked her dad where it really counts. (*Ouch*) But instead of brushing it off or laughing, he blew up. He jumped up, yelled a few choice words, and stormed off, leaving the girls looking stunned and hurt. It was heartbreaking. He'd set the playful tone, but when things went south, he flipped the script entirely. What are those girls supposed to think the next time they want to play with their dad? They're probably going to think twice before getting too rowdy again.

Consistency in parenting isn't just about keeping your mood in check (though that's a biggie); it's also about being consistent in discipline. It's important for parents to dish out calm and steady consequences, instead of knee-jerk punishments driven by the heat of the moment. We've all been there—handing out a punishment that was more about our own frustration than about teaching a lesson, something so over-the-top that we later realize, "Uh-oh, how am I going to enforce this?"

Why is this a problem for consistent parenting? Because when we fail to follow through, we undermine the trust and stability that children need. It sends mixed messages about what's really expected of them and whether the rules are actually important. Consistent discipline helps children understand the boundaries of acceptable behavior and the consequences when they cross those lines. It builds a sense of security, knowing that their parents' responses are predictable and fair. When we rely on consistency rather than emotion to guide our parenting, we create an environment where children feel safe to explore, make mistakes, and learn from them, confident that the rules and consequences will be applied fairly every time.

## REFLECTION QUESTIONS:

- Have you ever given your child a consequence based purely on emotion—like declaring *"No TV for a month!"* —only to realize later it's unrealistic to enforce? What led to that reaction?

- Why is it problematic for consistent parenting when consequences are driven by emotion rather than thoughtful boundaries? How might it affect your child's understanding of rules and expectations?

- How do you handle situations where you've given a consequence you can't follow through on? Do you adjust the consequence or stick with it to maintain consistency?

- What strategies can help you stay calm and set fair, enforceable boundaries, even in the heat of the moment?

# CHAPTER 22

## DEALING WITH A BAD HAND

Every Thursday morning, like clockwork, I give my parents a call to check in on their Wednesday night poker session. Without fail, my mother kicks off the conversation with, "The cards were terrible," and then my father chimes in with something charmingly blunt like, "Don't blame the cards; it's the way you play 'em." Classic husband-wife banter. But there's a nugget of wisdom in there: *You can't control the hand you're dealt, but you can absolutely control how you play it.* Turns out, you have a lot more influence over your success than you might think.

As parents, we often feel like we're dealt a tough hand—maybe it's a child who just won't sleep through the night or potty train. It's easy to chalk it up to bad luck or an unfortunate phase of life. But here's the thing: There's usually more we can do to improve the situation than we realize. The moment we throw our hands up and say, "I guess this is just how it is," we're essentially handing over all the control to our children and missing out on an opportunity to steer things in a better direction.

I've seen this play out in therapy sessions, too. Clients will tell me, "I can't change," or, even more disheartening, "They'll never change." And I can't help but wonder, if that's really what they believe, what is the benefit of therapy? It's like they've already decided to give up and, in doing so, given themselves—or someone else—permission to stay stuck.

This mindset reminds me of those poker players who grumble, "I NEVER get good cards," or, "I NEVER win." That's a classic case of "catastrophizing," where you turn every situation into a disaster and assume the worst is always going to happen. Let's be real—saying something *never* happens is almost always an exaggeration. It's a way to justify why things aren't going well, without having to admit that maybe, just maybe, we need to up our game. Think about how ridiculous that statement would sound if you said, "I NEVER hit a red light," or "I NEVER burn my toast." We both know that's not true—especially the toast part.

Children are pros at catastrophizing, too. I hear these kinds of statements daily: "You never buy me anything," "We never have anything good for dinner," or my personal favorite, "You never play with me." The list goes on. It's as if these over-the-top statements help them rationalize their feelings, which can then lead to a misplaced sense of entitlement. If we let our children believe these exaggerations, they'll start to expect the world to revolve around their skewed perceptions.

When my children throw a catastrophized statement my way, I like to challenge it. I'll ask, "Is it really true that I've never bought you anything? Never made a dinner you like? Never played with you?" Spoiler alert: the answer is usually "No." Then I'll say, "Okay, since that's not true, let's drop those kinds of statements." I want them to express their feelings in a way that's honest and grounded in reality, not driven by hyperbole. It's crucial for us as parents to address these statements head-on, so we don't reinforce a mindset that leads to unrealistic expectations and entitlement.

REFLECTION QUESTIONS:

- What are some of the most memorable catastrophized statements your child has made—like *"I'll never be good at this!"* or *"This is the worst day ever!"*?

- What do you think motivates these dramatic declarations? Are they seeking attention, expressing frustration, or trying to communicate feelings they don't yet have the words for?

- How do you typically respond when your child makes these statements? Do you validate their feelings, help them gain perspective, or both?

- What strategies can help your child learn to express their emotions in a balanced way without minimizing their feelings?

# CHAPTER 23

## FOLLOW THROUGH

Ever heard the saying, "Don't let your mouth write a check your butt can't cash"? Sure, it's a little cheeky, but it's pure genius when it comes to nailing the concept of accountability. It's all about how easy it is to make promises—and how hard it can be to actually deliver on them.

Let's talk about Mike "The Mouth" Matusow, the poker player known as much for his trash talk as for his skills at the table. Plenty of athletes have been known for their banter too, and that's all well and good—as long as they can back it up with their performance. But here's where it gets tricky for us parents: sometimes, we end up making promises we can't keep, even if we didn't mean to.

We've all been there, right? You lay down the law, telling your child, "If you don't eat your vegetables, no dessert for you!" But then life happens—maybe you get distracted —and suddenly, dessert is back on the table, mess or no mess. Or maybe you promise, "If you're good all week, we'll go to the zoo on Saturday!" Then Saturday rolls around, and you're like, "Zoo? What zoo?" Whatever the case, not following through chips away at the trust your child has in you.

Here's the thing: if a child truly believes there won't be any dessert if they don't finish their dinner, you can bet they'll be more likely to eat it. But if they know you're a softie who won't follow through, they'll probably skip dinner and still hit you up for dessert later. (Not that I'd know anything about that, of course—*ahem*.) The same goes for something like picking up toys—if they believe a trip to the park is on the line, those toys will practically fly into that toy box like they're on a mission.

I remember when my daughter was four, and she unleashed a full-blown, Oscar-worthy tantrum at daycare. As her well-deserved consequence, we decided to pull the plug on her tablet time for three whole days. It seemed like solid parenting at the moment—until I realized we were headed to my parents' place that weekend, a solid three-and-a-half-hour-long drive away. Now, I don't know if you've ever been in a car with a 4-year-old, but if you have, you know that tablets are lifesavers, especially on long car rides. So, after two days, she got the tablet back. Naturally, my daughter noticed the sudden change in policy, and I could almost see the gears turning in her little head: "Hmm, so mom doesn't always mean what she says." Not exactly the lesson in consistency I was going for!

Following through can be a real challenge. It's just too hard to leave the store when your child's mid-tantrum, turning heads like a tiny, angry tornado. Or maybe you crumble when they hit you with those big, sad *Puss in Boots* eyes and say, "But I'm starving!"—as if they didn't just refuse dinner an hour ago.

But here's the thing: just like a poker player loses all credibility if they can't back up their trash talk with some serious card skills, every time we don't follow through on what we said we'd do, we're basically handing our credibility over to our children on a silver platter. And let's face it, once they know we're bluffing, they'll keep calling our bluff every single time.

## REFLECTION QUESTIONS:

- Can you recall any promises your parents made to you—big or small—that they either kept or didn't follow through on? How did that affect your trust in them or shape your expectations?

- What promises have you made to your own children, and how consistent have you been in keeping them?

- How do you think keeping (or breaking) promises impacts your child's sense of security and trust in your relationship?

- What steps can you take to ensure that the promises you make are realistic and that your follow-through strengthens your bond with your children?

# CHAPTER 24

## ALL IN THE DETAILS

In poker, every player knows that when it comes to making a bet, the devil is in the details. You've got to weigh what's at stake and decide if your hand is strong enough to make it worth the risk. Without knowing exactly what you stand to lose—or gain—you're basically flying blind, like a bat trying to navigate through a disco party. And honestly, the same goes for parenting.

When it comes to implementing consequences, being *specific* is key. Children need to know exactly what's going to happen if they keep pushing those buttons. Saying something like, "If you keep that up, you'll be in trouble," is just too vague. "In trouble" could mean anything from losing a toy to being grounded to just getting a disapproving look from across the room and nothing more. If the consequences are unclear, your child might decide it's worth the gamble to keep up the mischief.

But here's the thing: being clear about consequences can save you a ton of headaches, especially as your children get older. Teenagers, in particular, seem to have a natural knack for arguing the fine print. If you say, "I'm taking your phone away," they'll want to know for how long. If you say, "You're grounded," they'll ask about parole for good behavior. And honestly, who can blame them? No one likes indefinite consequences, and it's a lot harder to behave well if you have no idea when or how you might get a break.

Think about it like this: in the justice system, inmates usually know how long they're in for and that good behavior could shave some time off their sentence. The same principle can work wonders with children. Clear, specific consequences not only help them understand the rules but also build trust. They'll know that when you say something, you mean it—and they'll be more likely to respect that.

Now, as I mentioned before, my iPhone alarm is one of my best-kept not-so-secret secrets. I'll tell my child, "You've got 10 more minutes to play with your train set, and then we'll brush your teeth." Then I set the alarm, and when it goes off, we're done. No arguments, no guessing—just clear expectations.

I've lost count of how many times I've heard parents at playdates say, "We're leaving in a few minutes," only for those "few minutes" to turn into an hour. How can your child learn to trust what you say if you don't stick to your word? Bottom line: if you say you're going to do something, do it. Otherwise, it's better not to say anything at all.

Let me share a little parenting misfire of my own. When my oldest son was 11, he dove headfirst into the world of video games. We had a Nintendo Switch and a couple of other systems—I couldn't tell you which ones because, well, my gaming expertise stops at knowing Mario drives around a cart. Anyway, one day, he earned himself a "no gaming" consequence. Later, I caught him glued to his tablet, happily playing a game. Naturally, I swooped in, ready to drop the parental hammer. His response? "But you said no *gaming*, not no tablet." *Touché, my son.* Apparently, in his world, "gaming" was strictly console territory, while tablets were a loophole in my parenting contract. It was a classic case of me not being clear enough, and it taught me an important lesson: when it comes to children, always close the loopholes.

REFLECTION QUESTIONS:

- What details do you think are most important to clarify with your child when it comes to setting specific consequences? How do you ensure they understand the connection between their actions and the outcomes?

- Have you ever faced a situation where a lack of clarity around consequences led to confusion, frustration, or inconsistency? How did that affect your child's behavior and your ability to enforce boundaries?

- How can you improve the way you communicate expectations and consequences to avoid misunderstandings in the future?

- What role does consistency play in helping your child learn from their actions, and how do you maintain that consistency even in challenging moments?

Detailed communication is also important. Try to avoid using "you" statements, which can come off as aggressive. Even though you're the parent, children feel more secure when they think they have some control. Instead of barking, "You need to clean your room!" try saying, "Please clean your room." We tell our children to be polite, but how often do we model that in how we talk to them? They're watching us, and if we want them to learn respectful communication, we've got to show them how it's done.

Another strategy for detailed communication with your child to facilitate the best responses or reactions is to tell them the behaviors you want to see rather than the behaviors you don't want to see. For example, instead of saying, "Stop leaving your toys all over the place," say, "Please put your toys back in the toy box." Instead of, "Stop bugging your sister," try, "I'd like you to sit quietly next to your sister." Communicate with your child in a way that directs them toward appropriate behavior rather than just acknowledging the behavior you don't want to see.

REFLECTION QUESTIONS:

- Have you noticed a change in your child's behavior when your communication is less aggressive and more calm or empathetic? How does their response differ in those moments?

- What happens when you're more detailed about what you *want* them to do instead of just pointing out what they're doing wrong? Does clearer guidance lead to better cooperation?

- How does your tone and choice of words influence the outcome of difficult conversations with your child?

- What communication strategies have you found most effective in encouraging positive behavior while maintaining respect and understanding?

# CHAPTER 25

## CLEAR COMMUNICATIONS

In poker, the consequences for losing a hand are pretty straightforward: you walk away with a lighter wallet and maybe a bruised ego. But when it comes to parenting, finding an equally effective consequence isn't always so clear-cut. What works wonders one day might fall flat the next, and what sends one child into line might barely register with another.

The key, though, is making sure that whatever consequence you choose is clearly communicated. As parents, we've got to use our best judgment and experience to figure out what's going to be most effective in any given situation. It's crucial for a child to understand exactly what they're up against if they decide to keep pushing those boundaries. Take my youngest son, for example—when he was 5, getting him out of bed in the morning was like trying to wake a hibernating bear. He knew that if he didn't get up, he'd miss out on his beloved granola bar and head to daycare on an empty stomach. That consequence was crystal clear to him, and it got results.

Another strategy I've used is the good old 1-2-3 system. It's simple but effective. "1" is the first warning—a gentle nudge that they need to change their behavior. "2" is the second warning, and now they know that if they don't shape up, there's going to be a consequence. "3" is the final call, and then the consequence kicks in, no ifs, ands, or buts.

But here's where things get a little tricky: context matters. Sometimes, you've got to think about the bigger picture. Let's say your child is really looking forward to a pool party at the end of the week. If they're slacking on chores or being disrespectful, that party can be powerful leverage. You can warn them that their pool party privileges are on the line if their behavior doesn't improve. But—and this is a big but—never threaten a consequence you're not willing or able to enforce. I've heard parents throw out lines like, "If you don't behave, Santa won't come this year," knowing full well that Santa's already scheduled his visit. If you're not going to follow through, it's best not to make the threat in the first place.

I remember a time when a parent threatened to "cancel Christmas" if their child didn't straighten up. Now, I'm pretty sure Christmas came just the same, because, let's be honest, no one's really going to cancel Christmas. But that kind of empty threat can do more harm than good. Your credibility as a parent is on the line. If your children catch on that you're bluffing, they'll start to tune out your warnings altogether. So, if you know deep down that you'd never actually follow through with a particular consequence, it's better to leave that threat on the shelf with the Elf.

In the end, clearly communicated consequences help set the stage for better behavior and a more trusting relationship with your child. It's all about being consistent, specific, and, most importantly, credible.

# CHAPTER 26

## NAG, NAG, NAG

Have you ever been called a nag? It's not exactly the kind of label anyone wants to wear. Nagging is when you try to change someone's behavior by repeating the same request over and over, hoping that eventually, they'll get the message. But let's be honest—if you find yourself nagging, or if someone's accused you of being a nag, then you might be part of the problem, too. If you've asked your child to do something once or twice and they're still ignoring you, it's probably time to switch gears and make it clear that a consequence is coming.

For instance, if you've asked your child to put their toys in the toybox and they're still scattered across the floor after the first, second, or even third request, it's time to lay down the law. Let them know that if those toys aren't picked up, they're going away—simple as that. And if you end up having to put the toys away yourself, well, the consequence is losing those toys. No need for nagging. If you keep making the same request without following through, your child (or anyone, really) will figure out pretty quickly that they don't have to take you seriously.

I remember when I was a teen, my mother had this Sunday morning routine of trying to get us up for church. She'd come into our rooms, tell us to get up, and then leave, only to come back again a few minutes later to repeat the same thing. I'd stay in bed as long as possible, thinking that if I just waited it out, we'd miss church, and I could keep sleeping. It wasn't until she finally said we'd be grounded if we didn't get up that I found the motivation to drag myself out of bed. When I didn't have the internal drive to get up, she had to introduce a consequence to create that motivation. And, spoiler alert: the potential of being grounded did the trick.

So, what's the deal with nagging, anyway? Why do we feel the need to repeat ourselves over and over? And what's the downside of doing it? Well, nagging can actually be counterproductive. The more you repeat yourself without any follow-through, the less your words seem to matter. Your requests start to feel like background noise, and the person you're trying to reach becomes more and more likely to tune you out. It's like they start to believe that if they ignore you long enough, they won't have to do what you're asking at all.

REFLECTION QUESTIONS:

- Even if you dislike the term, have you ever caught yourself nagging your child—repeating the same request over and over until frustration sets in? What situations tend to trigger this behavior?

- Why do you think parents often feel the need to repeat themselves? Is it out of fear of being ignored, frustration from past experiences, or a desire for immediate compliance?

- What's the downside of nagging—for both you and your

child? How might it affect your relationship, their sense of responsibility, or their motivation to follow through?

- What alternative strategies could help you communicate expectations more effectively without falling into the nagging trap?

# CHAPTER 27

## NO WORK, NO PAY

Ever seen a poker player collect their chips before winning the hand? Of course not. Why? Because they haven't earned it yet. It's a simple, unbreakable rule: you get the reward *after* you've done the work. This is a golden lesson for parents when it comes to promising rewards for completed tasks—and notice I said *completed* tasks. It's crucial not to jump the gun and reward your children before the job is done, because once they've got the reward in hand, their motivation to finish the job can vanish faster than you can say "clean your room." Just like most of us don't see a paycheck until the end of the pay period, children shouldn't get their rewards until their work is finished, for exactly the same reason.

My husband and I learned this the hard way when we took our three children on a trip to Kansas City for a two night stay at Great Wolf Lodge, with the premise of course that when we returned home, they agreed to behave and do all their chores and yada yada yada. Well, once we got home, their tune changed and we had no authority because they already got their reward.

A similar thing happened to me in high school. My mother bought me a gorgeous embroidered lavender prom dress, with the agreement that I'd work 20 hours to pay her back. Prom came and went, but I still had a bunch of hours left to work off. My motivation to finish those hours? Practically non-existent. It took a lot of effort from my mother to get me to fulfill the rest of my commitment.

As parents, it's important to understand that motivation can take a nosedive once a reward is in hand. Knowing this, we need to be creative and find ways to keep that motivation alive, even after the reward is earned.

REFLECTION QUESTIONS:

- Have you ever rewarded your child prematurely—
  offering praise, treats, or privileges before they fully
  completed a task? What led you to offer the reward early?

- How did your child respond? Did they follow through
  and finish the task, or did their motivation fade once the
  reward was given?

- What did you learn from that experience about the
  timing of rewards and its impact on motivation?

- How can you adjust your reward system to ensure it
  encourages follow-through and reinforces the value of
  effort and persistence?

# CHAPTER 28

## VALIDATING LANGUAGE

Who doesn't love a little praise after winning a poker hand? A simple "Great hand!" or "Nice play!" can go a long way in boosting someone's mood. The same goes for parenting. One of the most powerful tools in your parenting toolkit is learning how to use validating language with your child. Think about it—if you get frustrated when your feelings aren't validated, imagine how your child feels when they're not heard. Validating their feelings doesn't mean you're letting them off the hook, but it shows that you're listening and that their emotions are important.

Take the classic dinnertime struggle: your child declares, "I hate carrots!" Instead of brushing it off or insisting they eat them anyway, you can acknowledge their feelings. You might say, "I know you don't like carrots; it's hard to eat something you don't enjoy." This doesn't mean they get a free pass on eating vegetables, but it does mean they feel heard and understood. The expectation remains—they still need to eat their veggies—but now they know you're on their side, even if they're not thrilled about it.

THE POKER PLAYER'S GUIDE TO PARENTING   189

Validating language can also be a lifesaver during those morning school blues. When my son grumbles about going to school, I try to empathize. I might say, "I get it, sometimes I don't feel like going to work either. Staying home sounds pretty great, doesn't it? But hey, let's plan something fun for the weekend—what do you want to do when we have time to just relax?" This way, I'm not changing the expectation that he goes to school, but I'm showing him that I understand how he feels. Plus, it gives him something to look forward to, which can make the idea of getting through the school day a bit easier.

Even when you disagree with your child, validating their feelings can make a big difference. It's important to let them know that it's okay to have a different opinion. This is especially crucial when dealing with sibling disagreements. My children can argue about anything—like which color is better, pink or blue. In those moments, I try to help them see that it's okay to have different favorite colors. Just because one of them loves pink doesn't mean blue is any less awesome. By validating both of their opinions, I'm teaching them that it's okay to disagree and that they don't have to convince each other to see things the same way.

REFLECTION QUESTIONS:

- How does your child respond when you use validating language—acknowledging their feelings, frustrations, or achievements without judgment?

- Have you noticed any shifts in their mood or behavior after feeling understood and supported? Do they become calmer, more open, or more cooperative?

- How has using validation affected your overall

relationship with your child? Does it lead to deeper conversations or greater trust?

- What strategies can you use to incorporate more validating language into daily interactions, even during challenging moments?

# CHAPTER 29

## ANGER, OR IS IT

Let's talk about poker for a moment. Ever watched the reactions of players when they're knocked out of a game? Nine times out of ten, they're furious. Makes sense, right? But here's a thought: what if there's more going on beneath that angry facade? Maybe that player just lost the money they needed for their mortgage, and fear is creeping in. Or perhaps they're embarrassed, doubting their poker skills and feeling a bit vulnerable. There's a whole cocktail of emotions that could be in play, yet anger always seems to take center stage. But why? Is it because anger is the socially acceptable go-to? Or maybe it's a defense mechanism to keep vulnerability at bay? And let's not forget—sometimes, acting angry actually gets you what you want.

Now, take a look at your own children. Ever noticed how they react when they don't get their way? I remember taking my son to a parade and carnival when he was three. You'd think he'd be thrilled, right? But when it was time to leave, he was furious—face red, arms crossed, the whole nine yards. I was baffled. We'd had such a great time, and here he was, ending it on an angry note.

But if I dig a little deeper, was it really just anger? Or was he maybe feeling disappointed that the fun was over and didn't know how to express it?

For whatever reason, anger is socially acceptable and, let's face it, sometimes even rewarded (insert Will Smith slap joker here). Had we given in and stayed at the carnival, we'd have been teaching him that anger is the magic key to getting what he wants. And you know what happens when behavior is rewarded—it gets repeated.

As a parent, it's tempting to just say no to the compliant child and avoid the tantrum altogether. But what if, instead of just reacting to the anger, we tried to understand it? Maybe asking, "What's got you so upset?" could open up a conversation. It's important for children to know it's okay to feel angry, and that anger itself isn't the problem— it's how they handle it that matters. Saying something like, "I'd be angry too if that happened," can go a long way in validating their feelings without encouraging bad behavior.

Anger is often justified, but what follows it can be less so. By figuring out what's really going on, we can help our children work through their emotions and find a better way to deal with them.

So, can you relate to the shame that sometimes sneaks in with anger? Ever noticed that anger is often just the tip of the emotional iceberg? And how do you handle it when your children are righteously angry? Have you found ways to help them—and maybe even yourself—uncover what's really going on underneath?

When something's visibly off with me, or if I'm giving off those unmistakable angry vibes without actually saying what's got me riled up, I've coached my husband to ask, "Are you mad at me, or is it something else?" Spoiler: it's usually not him. Most of the time, I'm just using anger as a shield to dodge my actual feelings, or worse, I'm projecting that anger onto him when he's not even the culprit. And let's be real, if grown-ups like us have a hard time communicating when we're angry, what hope do our children have?

I'd argue that anger is often a defense mechanism, a way to protect ourselves from emotions that make us feel, well, vulnerable.

Take this scenario: your child says something mean, and instead of acknowledging that it stings, you lash out in anger. Why? Because admitting it hurts would mean showing vulnerability, and who wants to do that? But here's the catch—if our children see us dodging emotional hurt and covering it up with anger, they're probably going to pick up that same habit. I sometimes wonder if parents avoid vulnerability because they fear it gives their children the upper hand. But here's the thing: vulnerability doesn't equal weakness.

Imagine a poker player loses a game and bursts into tears. Awkward, right? But if that same player throws down their cards, shoves their chair back, and yells something unrepeatable? No one would bat an eye. I once talked to a college football player who said it was pretty normal for guys to punch holes in walls when they were mad. But crying to a buddy? Now that's where it gets socially unacceptable. So, why is it that showing emotional vulnerability is so out of the norm?

We live in a culture that reinforces angry behavior because being emotionally open is seen as weak. But is anger really that powerful? If getting mad gets you what you want, then maybe it does feel powerful, and that's why we keep going back to it.

REFLECTION QUESTIONS:

- Can you think of any instances where anger—whether yours or your child's—was used as a tool to get what was wanted? What was the outcome of that approach?

- Have there been moments when you or your child bypassed vulnerability and went straight to anger instead of expressing deeper emotions like fear, sadness, or frustration?

- How has this pattern affected communication and problem-solving within your family?

- What strategies could help you or your child feel safe enough to express vulnerability instead of defaulting to anger?

# CHAPTER 30

## CONTRIBUTION TO THE POT

I remember being green with envy as a child, watching my friends rake in their weekly allowances. Imagine getting money just for existing—what a sweet deal! But now that I'm on the other side of the parenting fence (and a therapist to boot), I can confidently say that allowances might just be the WORST. IDEA. EVER. Seriously, they're like the express lane to Entitlement City, and we're handing out tickets left and right.

Allowances send a pretty clear message: you get something for nothing. And while that might sound like a dream come true when you're 10, it's a nightmare waiting to happen as they grow up. We wonder why younger generations are often accused of feeling entitled—well, allowances could be one of the culprits. The expectation that money will just magically appear with no effort? That's a dangerous mindset.

Think about a poker tournament. You can't just waltz in and expect to play without putting some money into the pot, right? There's a buy-in, and that's how it should work. Parenting isn't all that different. I see it as a fee-for-service arrangement: you complete a chore or good behavior, you get a reward. Just like in the real world. No contribution, no pot—simple as that.

Handing out allowances with no strings attached is like printing a one-way ticket to entitlement. Children start expecting rewards for nothing, and that's a tough habit to break. If they learn early on that money (or any reward, really) comes as a result of effort, we're setting them up for a much healthier relationship with work and rewards.

REFLECTION QUESTIONS:

- What's your perspective on giving allowances—do you see them as a tool for teaching responsibility or as something that risks creating entitlement?

- Have you noticed any signs of entitlement in your child as a result of receiving an allowance? How do you address those moments when they arise?

- In what ways might you, as a parent, unintentionally feed into feelings of entitlement—whether through rewards, leniency, or meeting every request?

- How do you handle allowances in your household? Are they tied to chores, behavior, or given as a way to teach financial management? What's worked (or not worked) for your family?

# CHAPTER 31

## INEVITABILITY OF LOSING

Let's face it—no one in the history of poker has won every single time. Some players might have better streaks than others, but not a single one can claim an undefeated record. The same goes for parenting. There are parents who seem to have it all figured out, but even they have lost a few battles here and there. Just like poker players need to check themselves when they lose (and not just when they win), parents need to be mindful of how they handle their own losses and how they teach their children to handle theirs.

When our oldest son was 6 and our daughter was 3, we played a lot of games together. Our son was just starting to understand that losing is part of the game. Sure, it's not fun, but you've got to roll with it. Our daughter, on the other hand, was still stuck in the "losing is the end of the world" phase. If she didn't win, the pout would come out, and she'd flat-out refuse to keep playing. In her mind, not winning was the same as not getting what she wanted, and there was no way to see that sticking it out could lead to a win later.

One time, we were playing musical pillows—a spin on musical chairs because, well, we didn't have enough chairs. I was on piano duty, playing tunes while my husband, son, and daughter circled the pillows. When the music stopped, they'd race to grab one of the two pillows on the floor. At first, my husband was letting the children win, but I nudged him to step up his game and see how they'd handle a loss. Sure enough, when my daughter didn't get a pillow, she pouted and stomped off.

So, what's a parent to do? It's tempting to let her win and avoid the drama, but that's not really winning, is it? If we don't let our children experience loss, we miss out on teaching them that losing happens, and how you handle it is just as important as winning. Sure, it's okay to validate their disappointment, but we shouldn't smooth over every bump in the road. If she chose to pout, she had to sit out until she was ready to play without the attitude. That day, she decided to change her behavior and came back to play, which I chalked up as a parenting win.

But why is losing so hard for us to accept, even though we all know no one wins all the time? Is it because it makes us feel vulnerable? Does it shake up how we see ourselves and our worth? Or maybe it forces us to face the music about how we could do better. I don't have all the answers, but I do know that helping our children learn to cope with losing is crucial. If we don't, those small losses could turn into bigger problems down the road.

REFLECTION QUESTIONS:

- Do you ever let your children win at games just to avoid a meltdown or keep the peace? What's your reasoning behind those choices?

- How do your children react when you genuinely win—do they handle it gracefully, or does frustration take over?

THE POKER PLAYER'S GUIDE TO PARENTING   199

- Do you believe there's value in allowing your child to experience a loss? What lessons do you think losing can teach them about resilience, sportsmanship, and perseverance?

- How do you help your child process those losses in a way that builds their confidence rather than discouraging them from trying again?

# CHAPTER 32

## SELECTIVE SHARING

Let's talk about my father and his poker nights. Thursday morning, I'd get a call from him, and it usually went something like this: "Guess what? I won big last night!" Naturally, I started to think he was some kind of poker genius, winning all the time. But then it dawned on me—he wasn't calling every Thursday, just the ones after a winning night. Turns out, he was a master of selective sharing, only reaching out when there was good news to report. I assumed he was always winning because, well, that's all I ever heard about.

This got me thinking about my children and their after-school reports. They come home all smiles, sharing the highlights of their day, and I'm left thinking everything's peachy. But I've come to realize that, just like my father, they're not telling me everything. They're not exactly lining up to volunteer the not-so-great parts. After all, who really wants to dive into a conversation about something that might be uncomfortable or embarrassing? My father sure doesn't want to call me on a Thursday morning just to say he lost last night. I mean, who would? It's like dialing up disappointment on purpose.

THE POKER PLAYER'S GUIDE TO PARENTING    201

There was this one time when our son was invited to a birthday party at a friend's house. My husband went to pick him up, and what started as a fun day turned into a full-blown meltdown. As a side note, our son and my husband were supposed to go fishing after the party. As our son was picked up, he didn't want to leave, so he threw himself on the ground, launched his toys, and screamed about how "boring" fishing was when my husband reminded him that they were going after the party. By the time they got home, my husband was so hurt, I could see it all over his face. So, I went in to talk to our son, who by then had cooled down and was starting to understand just how badly he'd behaved. As I moved his beloved Transformers out of his room—his favorite toys—he knew this wasn't going to be just a chat. There were consequences, and no fishing trip for him. My husband took our daughter instead, and our son got to clean up the basement toy room. It was a tough lesson, but one we had to go through.

A few days later, we were out running errands and drove by his friend's house—the scene of the meltdown. My husband brought it up, and before I could say anything, our son slapped his hands over his face and begged, "Can we please not talk about it?" That moment hit me. It's hard to face up to moments where we've felt embarrassed or have to own up to our actions. Whether it's my son not wanting to talk about his meltdown or my father skipping the Thursday calls after a loss, there's a common thread: we all want to avoid uncomfortable conversations. But just because it's tough doesn't mean we should skip it. Avoidance might feel better in the short term, but it doesn't teach us much.

This experience reminded me how crucial it is to hold ourselves —and our children—accountable. Sure, it's tempting to avoid those tough talks, but by doing so, are we reinforcing the idea that it's okay to dodge accountability? If I had let my son off the hook when he didn't want to talk about his meltdown, I'd have spared him some discomfort, but at what cost? Would he have learned anything? Would his behavior have changed? Probably not.

Accountability isn't supposed to be easy, but it's a necessary part of growth. And as uncomfortable as it might be, it's important for my son—and for all of us—to learn to face it. So, even if my father didn't win at poker on Wednesday night, I hope he knows he can still give me a call on Thursday. We don't always have to talk about wins—sometimes the best lessons come from the losses.

REFLECTION QUESTIONS:

- Can you recall a time when your child tried to avoid a conversation about accountability because it made them uncomfortable? What was the situation, and how did you recognize their discomfort?

- How did you handle the conversation—did you push through, give them space, or approach it from a different angle?

- What strategies have you found effective in encouraging open and honest discussions about responsibility without overwhelming your child?

- How do you balance holding your child accountable while also creating a safe space for them to learn from their mistakes?

# CHAPTER 33

## PROJECTION

I'm going to go out on a limb here and assume that unless they're winning, poker players are probably a moody bunch. I mean, how could they not be? The odds are rarely in their favor, and even when they do win, it's not like everyone else is throwing them a parade. Now, here's another safe bet: children are moody too. But the thing about poker players and children is that you can't always give them what they want just to keep them happy. (And if you're in the habit of doing that with your children, well, we've got a whole other set of issues to discuss.)

When you're in a foul mood or just plain frustrated with something, it's tough to keep those feelings neatly packed away. The frustration with one thing tends to spill over into everything else. Picture a poker player who's just had a lousy hand. It's pretty hard for them to keep that frustration bottled up and only directed at the cards. Before you know it, the dealer, the other players, and even the next hand are all catching some of that leftover anger.

Now, let's be honest, the same thing happens at home—whether it's the children, the parents, or both. After a rough day at school or work, it's nearly impossible to compartmentalize all those feelings and only take them out on the source of the frustration. Whether it's reacting to a bad hand in poker or a bad day at the office, projection onto innocent bystanders—like your family—is all too common in both poker and parenting.

I remember when my son was 7, he got really into drawing. He was all about creating these intricate pictures of his favorite Transformers or comic book heroes. One day, while he was deep into a drawing, he made a mistake. He got so frustrated that he bolted out of his chair, marched into the living room, and shoved his sister, who was just sitting there minding her own business. His frustration with the drawing had nothing to do with her, but she ended up on the receiving end of it.

So, what did I do? Well, first, I told him he was losing two of his chips for acting out like that. Then, I sat him down and asked him to explain why he was so frustrated. I reassured him that I was there to help him figure things out, so he wouldn't feel the need to take his anger out on his sister. After our chat, I gave him an eraser, and we worked together to fix the mistake on his drawing. He was able to get back to his artwork, and his sister was saved from any more unfair shoves.

The thing is, learning to manage emotions—whether you're 7 or 37—takes time and practice. But if you don't give yourself, or your children, the chance to practice, nothing's going to change. The frustration will keep spilling over, and projection will keep happening.

REFLECTION QUESTIONS:

- How can you, as a parent, create opportunities for emotional regulation—both for yourself and your children—to help prevent emotional projection during stressful moments?

- Can you think of times when you've unintentionally projected your own emotions, like stress or frustration, onto others? What were the triggers, and how did it affect your interactions?

- Have you noticed your child projecting their own emotions onto you or their siblings? What patterns stand out, and how do you typically respond?

- What strategies can you use to help your child recognize when they're projecting emotions, and how can you guide them toward healthier ways of expressing their feelings?

# CHAPTER 34

## TRAUMA RESPONSE

L et's dive into the concept of a "bad beat." In poker, it's that hand you were so sure you'd win, only to lose in a twist of cruel fate. It's not just any loss—it's the kind that stings a little more because it blindsides you. The emotions tied to that loss can be intense, whether it's at the poker table or in life. When we encounter a loss, especially one we didn't see coming, the emotional response can be powerful and lingering. Trauma, in this sense, is the emotional fallout from an event so distressing that it overwhelms our ability to cope, leaving us feeling helpless, diminished, and sometimes disconnected from our own emotions.

Trauma doesn't just mess with our heads—it impacts our decision-making, too. Think about it: if a poker player suffers a bad beat with a particular hand, they might be hesitant to bet the same way next time, even if the odds are in their favor. It's a way of protecting themselves from feeling that same gut-wrenching disappointment again. But this protective instinct isn't just for poker players; it's something we all do, especially as parents.

Let me share a story about a mother I once spoke with. She had a child with a rare genetic disorder, a condition that arose from the combination of her and her husband's genetics. Her child was born at just 25 weeks and faced a lifetime of medical challenges. The experience was so traumatic that the couple decided not to have more children, fearing the possibility of going through the same ordeal again. Their trauma shaped their decision-making, driven by a desire to protect themselves and their child from more heartache.

Now, my own experience is on a much smaller scale, but it still left a mark. When my children were 7, 5, and 1, we were gearing up for Christmas when my youngest was diagnosed with RSV. If you've ever been in that position, you know how terrifying it is to watch your baby struggle to breathe. We were told to monitor him closely, especially at night, because things could go south quickly. The news was filled with stories of children being hospitalized—and worse—so you can imagine the fear that took hold of us.

At first, my responses were grounded in reality. My son was sick, and we did everything we could to help him recover: breathing treatments, steam showers, humidifiers—you name it, we did it. He slept in our arms so we could keep an eye on his breathing, and we kept him home from daycare far longer than necessary. But then, something shifted. My fear started to take over, and suddenly, every little thing felt like a potential crisis. Even when he was well on the mend, I kept up the steam showers, wouldn't let him cry it out at night, and practically turned our home into a sterile zone. My trauma had taken the wheel, and it was driving us all a little crazy.

Looking back, I can see that my trauma response had both protective and limiting effects. On the one hand, my over-the-top vigilance probably did keep him from getting sick again. On the other hand, it cost us countless sleepless nights and drained a lot of our energy in ways that, in hindsight, weren't really necessary.

So here's the question I want you to think about: How much of our trauma is genuinely protective and based in reality, and how much of it is dysfunctional and fear-driven? My example shows both sides—yes, my actions may have helped, but they also went too far, fueled by fear rather than rationality.

What's the balance? When does a trauma response cross the line from being realistic to being extreme? And in what situations has your own trauma response influenced your decisions?

REFLECTION QUESTIONS:

- What does balance look like when it comes to trauma responses? How can you differentiate between a realistic, protective response and an extreme reaction rooted purely in fear?

- Can you think of situations where your own trauma response has influenced your decision-making as a parent? How did it affect the outcome?

- How do you recognize when fear is driving your actions instead of logic or reason? What strategies help you pause and reassess?

- In what ways can you model healthy coping mechanisms for your child, showing them how to respond to challenges without letting fear take control?

# CHAPTER 35

## CONCLUSION

There are endless ways to draw parallels between one of my favorite games, poker, and one of my greatest honors: being a parent to my three incredibly demanding, yet wonderfully amazing, children. Just as in poker, there are highs and lows, but we persevere. We persevere because we have so much riding on our success.

For me, winning at poker is gratifying, a tradition passed down through my family, shared with neighbors and moms, alike and is deeply ingrained in our shared experiences and values. Yet, as much as I enjoy the thrill of a poker victory, I find even greater fulfillment in succeeding as a parent. The stakes are higher, the challenges more profound, and the rewards infinitely more meaningful.

In both poker and parenting, strategic thinking, patience, and emotional resilience are crucial. Each game, each day with my children, presents unique scenarios that require me to adapt, learn, and grow. The victories in parenting may not come with trophies, but they are celebrated in the moments of joy, growth, and connection with my children.

Ultimately, the skills honed at the poker table—observing, strategizing, and maintaining composure under pressure—translate seamlessly into the realm of parenting. Both require a balance of intuition and logic, and both reward those who are committed to learning from their experiences and striving for improvement. In this intricate game of life, my ultimate win is seeing my children thrive and knowing that I played a part in their journey.

# EPILOGUE

As we reach the end of this journey together, I want to extend my heartfelt gratitude to you, the reader. *The Poker Player's Guide to Parenting* has been a labor of love, born from my passion for poker and my dedication to being the best parent I can be. Your decision to embark on this journey with me means more than words can express.

Throughout these pages, we've explored the fascinating parallels between the strategic world of poker and the unpredictable adventure of parenting. We've delved into the highs and lows—the moments of triumph and the challenges that test our resolve. My hope is that you've found insights, strategies, and perhaps a bit of inspiration to apply to your own parenting journey.

Parenting, much like poker, is a game of skill, patience, and intuition. It's about making the best possible decisions with the cards you're dealt and staying ready to adapt when the game changes. It's about celebrating the wins, learning from the losses, and cherishing the moments in between. As you continue your journey, remember: every hand you play, every decision you make as a parent, is part of a greater story. The lessons you learn and the experiences you share will shape not only your life but also the lives of your children.

Thank you for allowing me to be part of your journey. Your willingness to read, reflect, and engage with these ideas speaks to your commitment to being an extraordinary parent. May your path be filled with joy, growth, and countless winning hands.

*With gratitude,*
*Leaha Hammer, Author*